Fastest to Canada

Fastest to Canada

The *Royal Edward*:
from Govan to Gallipoli

Richard Oliff

· MARITIME HERITAGE ·
from
The NOSTALGIA Collection

This work is dedicated to my lovely Grandmother,
Mary Derry Westwood-Nimmo,
who was the inspiration for my research.

To my Great Uncle William Duncan Dick Nimmo,
who was lost, has been found and will never be forgotten.

And to all of those who lost their lives aboard
HMT *Royal Edward* on 13 August 1915.

© Richard Oliff 2004

All rights reserved. No part of this publication may be reproduced, stored in a retrieval system or transmitted, in any form or by any means, electronic, mechanical, photocopying, recording or otherwise, without prior permission in writing from Silver Link Publishing Ltd.

First published in 2004

British Library Cataloguing in Publication Data

A catalogue record for this book is available from the British Library.

ISBN 1 85794 233 7

Silver Link Publishing Ltd
The Trundle
Ringstead Road
Great Addington
Kettering
Northants NN14 4BW

Tel/Fax: 01536 330588
email: sales@nostalgiacollection.com
Website: www.nostalgiacollection.com

Printed and bound in Great Britain

Frontispiece **A poster by Odin Rosenvinge, to be seen in Bristol Industrial Museum, advertising the Royal Line, its boast being that its ships were the fastest to Canada. RMS *Royal Edward* is proudly portrayed. Bristol Industrial Museum is situated in the Floating Harbour in an old transit shed for goods coming into the city. Printing, flying, trains, cars, buses and ships are just some of the subjects to be experienced in a museum containing more than 700 exhibits relating to Bristol's long and varied industrial past.** *PTP*

Readers are invited to contact the author, via the publisher, with any further information about loved ones, additions, amendments, family photographs, memorabilia and thoughts, etc, for possible future editions of this book.

Contents

COMMONWEALTH WAR GRAVES COMMISSION

DEBT OF HONOUR REGISTER

In Memory of

WILLIAM DUNCAN DICK NIMMO

Fifth Engineer Officer
S.S. "Royal Edward" (Toronto), Mercantile Marine

who died on
Friday 13 August 1915 . Age 25 .

Additional Information:	Inter. Son of John and Isabella Watson Nimmo (nee Marshall), of 58, Church St., Coatbridge, Lanark. Born at Coatbridge.
Cemetery:	TOWER HILL MEMORIALLondon, United Kingdom
Visiting Information:	The Memorial Register may be consulted at Trinity House Corporation, Trinity Square (Cooper's Row entrance), which will be found behind the Memorial. Tel: 020 7481 6900

No roses

There are no roses on sailors' graves,
Nor wreaths upon the storm tossed waves,
No last post from the Royals' band,
So far away from their native land,
No heartbroken words carved on stone,
Just shipmates' bodies there alone,
The only tributes are the seagulls' sweeps,
And the teardrop when a loved one weeps.

Anon

'We can truly say that the whole circuit of the earth is girdled with the graves of our dead … and, in the course of my pilgrimage, I have many times asked myself whether there can be more potent advocates of peace upon earth through the years to come, than this massed multitude of silent witnesses to the desolation of war.'

His Majesty King George V, Flanders, 1922

Introduction

It dawned on me recently just how similar my early days had been to Thomas Hardy's Jude growing up in fictitious Wessex. Local, native, provincial, parochial, indigenous, regional and somewhat insular. God, how things have changed in such a short span of time! My mother used to tell me that time would fly when I travelled beyond the age of 21, but one has to get beyond that point to realise just how true a statement that is. Life is without doubt a short affair, yet thankfully this realisation is confined to those of experience and years. Trying to find a beginning to a tale is not as easy as I would have thought. Logic dictates that there can only be one beginning, despite the many beginnings and fresh starts that we all experience throughout life, so I guess I will start with my own beginning and take things from there.

I was, I'm fairly safe in saying, conceived in Corby, Northamptonshire, around August 1954, yet when it came to my birth my mother and I were carted off in an ambulance to the nearest town with a maternity hospital, Kettering. Accompanying us was a midwife by the name of Margaret Atkinson, who has since said that I was almost born in the back of said ambulance, such was the urgency.

My first breath was drawn at around seven o'clock on the evening of Monday 23 May 1955 at Saint Mary's Hospital on Kettering's London Road. In fact, most of my contemporaries from around the area made their first appearance within those disinfected walls. Today the hospital is a care home facility for the geriatric population of our small world. The thought of ending my days in the same building, blubbering and dribbling in much the same way as a baby, has a certain poetic, albeit desperately depressing, irony.

My family lived at 27 Thoroughsale Road in Corby, a semi-detached council-owned property on Corby's Lloyd's estate. This was to be my home for the first part of my trip through life. My mother was Isabella Marshall Watson, my father Digby Hugh. I was born the youngest of four children: my siblings are Louis John Thomas (great name – I'm sure my parents were having a laugh), Thomas Grainger, and my sister Elizabeth. I was destined to be forever referred to as the 'baby' of the family: how I hated that. I also disliked the fact that I was the only member of my family to have been born in a hospital as opposed to a home birth. I don't know why I hated this so much, I just did. Another thing that made me *different* from the rest was my left-handedness. My grandma would show me to the neighbours and they would hand things to me and gasp in amazement as I offered my preferred hand. This may seem somewhat tame today, but this was at a time when left-handed people were only just being accepted as 'normal'.

My grandmother used to tell me about her brother-in-law Willie (she used to refer to him as Uncle Willie when speaking to me) who was lost at sea during the First World War. She would talk about him with loving affection and always with a tear ready to fall – about how he was on a ship that sank many years ago. All I could do was to sit and listen, but not very well. You see, I loved my grandma dearly, but in 1970 I was only 15 years old with a head full of pop music trivia and the discovery of girls. I had tea with my grandma every Friday evening. It just became a habit – one of those things – but we both seemed to enjoy each other's company. Maybe there was some kind of synergy going on – you know, one on the threshold of an entire life and the other entering the Christmas of theirs. No one else, apart from grandma, had ever mentioned Willie. Maybe she was the last person to carry a light or memory for him.

My grandma had been born Mary Derry Westwood on 2 June 1887 at 31 Coats Street, Coatbridge, Scotland. Her father was George, a tube welder, who had married Elizabeth Norris in Coatbridge on 15 February 1869. Grandma married John Nimmo, an electrical engineer, who had a brother called Willie – or, to give him his full name, William Duncan Dick Nimmo. This was the Willie to whom my grandma had referred. He must have been a special man for my grandma to have remembered him with such affection.

My lovely grandma died on 29 June 1970 not long after her 83rd birthday. She had been a little girl, she had had her dreams, she had married, she had had five children who had all, in turn, married well, she had been surrounded by countless grandchildren, and she had died. I cried like a drain that day.

My family is a big family. I have cousins, second cousins and third cousins all over the world. My grandma was my mother's mother, and many from that side of my family had chosen, many years ago, to settle in Vancouver, Canada. This was the Nimmo side of the family. One of those to make the big move from Scotland to Canada was my grandma's sister-in-law Janet, who had married John Patterson. Janet, known affectionately to my mother as Aunt Jessie, had a daughter, Isabella; she was my mum's cousin, and married Alexander Munro. Confused? Well, I'm trying to keep it as simple as I can.

It was during my last trip to Vancouver in October 2002 that Alex and Isabel showed me a faded photocopy of a picture and obituary that had appeared in a Scottish newspaper way back in 1915. Next to this entry is a photograph of a young man wearing what appears to be a naval uniform of some description, standing on the deck of a ship. Since the picture I was looking at was a poor photocopy, it was difficult to make out any clear detail of the uniform, whether it was Royal Navy or Merchant Navy. Either way, he looked rather grand and handsome with his white peaked cap and his eight shiny buttons on his jacket. (I later discovered that these eight buttons denoted the rank of officer in the Canadian Mercantile Marine.)

His stance was very posed, hands in his jacket pockets, straight back, and his right foot on the bottom rung of a ship's stairway. Exactly which ship was not made clear, yet it is highly likely to have been the RMS *Royal Edward*. Underneath the photograph was the inscription 'I am not dead, but finished with this world'.

So, this was Willie. It was almost as if, after all those years, my grandma was sitting next to me saying, 'There's more to this story, you know.' But other than this newspaper entry, little more was known about this man, my grandfather's brother. I was intrigued.

When I returned from Vancouver I decided to research the detail, or as much as I could, from the limited information in the obituary. It was as if someone was pushing me to tell a complete story that surely couldn't be much more than the fact that here was a man who had died at sea during the First World War – just one of so many from so many different lands to lose their lives.

But what of the ship? What of the crew and passengers? And what had happened on the day that Willie and so many had died?

In Loving Memory
OF
WILLIAM DUNCAN DICK NIMMO,
WHO WENT HOME ON
H.M.T. Royal Edward, on 14th August, 1915.

HIS MESSAGE.

At my post, dear mother mine,
I have reached the Shore Divine,
God has answered clear your prayer,
He has kept me ever near.

What I've failed in, He'll forgive,
God in Heaven doth ever live,
Keep on praying mother dear,
He will answer every prayer.

Honour bright has been my aim,
I have never sought for fame,
Only answered duty's call,
Reached the everlasting goal.

Now dear mother, weep no more,
Since I've reached the Golden Shore;
God you trust, he'll never fail,
Till you're safe inside the veil.

Canadian MM Fifth Engineering Officer/2nd Lt RN
William Duncan Dick Nimmo, 1889-1915:
'I am not dead, but finished with this world'.
Author's collection

I have often looked at memorials to 'The Glorious Dead', which list row upon row of people who had fought and died for freedom, mostly during the two World Wars of the 20th century. It had never really occurred to me that each of those names represented a real living person with dreams, hopes and aspirations – individuals prematurely stopped in their tracks by death.

Behind each name on these cenotaphs to the brave there is a story. Sadly, most of the stories die with time, or even died at the time. But there was something inside me telling me to preserve the memory of my Great Uncle William and the hundreds of crew and soldiers who lost their lives on that fateful day. From Scotland to Avonmouth, Suffolk to Kettering, and from Canada to Nisyros in the Aegean, this story was to bring to life a once proud luxury passenger/troopship, some of the characters that sailed aboard her, and a tiny First World War German submarine.

1
The Nimmo family

William Duncan Dick Nimmo was born on 25 November 1889 in Coatbridge, Lanarkshire, Scotland. His parents, my great-grandparents, were John and Isabella Watson Nimmo (née Marshall). His four brothers were Gilbert Stewart, John (my grandfather), James and Thomas Grainger Marshall. His sisters included Janet, Isabella and Mary. William's father worked in the local steelworks, helping to produce the goods that fed the great Clyde shipbuilding industry.

At the turn of the last century Coatbridge was the eighth largest town in Scotland, having been formed by the amalgamation of a number of local villages: Old Monkland and Kirkshaws, Coatbridge, Coatdyke, Dundyvan, Gartsherrie, Langloan and Whifflet. (Willie's parents had married in Langloan on 16 July 1884.) As Coatbridge grew, its landscape changed from a country area to a crowded industrial town. In 1811 Old Monkland parish, which included Coatbridge, was recorded as having fewer than 6,000 inhabitants. By the mid-1800s the iron industry was predominant in the town, and when it achieved Burgh status in 1885 it was known as 'the Iron Burgh' and its population had increased to around 25,000. Today, the population is estimated at more than 48,000.

The following was said about Coatbridge in the latter part of the 19th century, around the time of Willie's birth:

'There is no worse place out of hell than that neighbourhood. At night the groups of blast furnaces on all sides might be imagined to be blazing volcanoes at most of which smelting is continued on Sundays and weekdays, day and night – without intermission.'

Today the older, heavy industries have almost disappeared and newer light industries are taking their place. Coatbridge has a number of attractions, including Summerlee Heritage Park – 'Scotland's noisiest museum' – and the Time Capsule leisure complex. It has a public baths, five railway stations – Coatdyke, Sunnyside, Blairhill, Central and Whifflet – many public parks, including the very popular Drumpellier Country Park with its Peace Garden, two golf courses, one cricket club, an indoor and outdoor sports centre, an indoor bowling centre, a ten pin bowling club, six industrial estates and a modern shopping centre. To quote the latest North Lanarkshire Official Guide, 'This vibrant town now boasts unrivalled leisure and entertainment facilities as well as ample shopping opportunities in the town centre precinct and retail parks.'

Drumpellier Park was gifted to the town by D. W. R. Carrick Buchanan in 1919. The Drumpellier estate can be traced back to 1161 and was the site of the original Grange built by the monks of Newbattle Abbey. The farming Grange,

Above left William's parents, John and Isabella Watson Nimmo, née Marshall, on the steps of their home in Church Street, Coatbridge. *Author's collection*

Above Another photograph of my great-grandparents, on the occasion of their Golden Wedding in 1934. *Author's collection*

Left Some of my Nimmo great-aunts and uncles: Gilbert Stewart, Thomas Grainger Marshall, John (my grandfather), Janet, James, and Mary. *Author's collection*

Baird Street, Coatbridge, in the early 1900s. Church Street runs across in front of the church. The carts are loading (or unloading) water and the kids seem to be enjoying it! At this time William would have been only an infant. The imposing church is Garsherrie Church, now known as St Andrew's. *Monklands Online*

Looking up Church Street, Coatbridge, towards St Andrew's from approximately where No 58 stood, on 14 June 2003. *Author*

Page 395.

BIRTHS in the _District_ of _Coatbridge_ in the _County_ of _Lanark_

No.	Name and Surname.	When and Where Born.	Sex.	Name, Surname, & Rank or Profession of Father. Name, and Maiden Surname of Mother. Date and Place of Marriage.	Signature and Qualification of Informant, and Residence, if out of the House in which the Birth occurred.	When and Where Registered, and Signature of Registrar.	
1183	Eliza Logue	1909. December Fourth 5h. 30m. a.m. Dundyvan Cottage Coatbridge	F	Daniel Logue Iron Work Labourer Eliza Logue m.s. Henry. 1886 July 24th Londonderry Ireland	Daniel Logue Father	1909. December 10th At Coatbridge James Mitchell Registrar	B
1184	Margaret Jane Docherty	1909. December Eighth 10 0m. a.m. 23 Baird Terrace Coatbridge	F	Henry Docherty Night Watchman Elizabeth Docherty m.s. Fegan 1891 January 31st Donegal Ireland	Henry Docherty Father present	1909. December 10th At Coatbridge James Mitchell Registrar	B
1185	William Duncan Dick Nimmo	1909. November Twenty fifth Noon. Alexandra Street Coatbridge	M	John Nimmo Tube Work Foreman Isabella Watson Nimmo m.s. Marshall 1884 July 16th Erskine Renfrewshire	J. W. Nimmo Mother	1909. December 10th At Coatbridge James Mitchell Registrar	B
					James Mitchell Registrar		

Left **The record of William's birth in 1889.**

Below left **My grandmother, Mary Derry Nimmo née Westwood (right), in about 1930 with her children (left to right) John (Jack), Isabella Watson Marshall (my mother), Elizabeth (Betty), May, and Thomas Grainger Marshall (Marshall).** *Author's collection*

which stood on the ridge near the site of Drumpellier House, was probably built from wood with a thatched roof. The monks cleared part of the extensive forest that covered the area at the time, cultivated the land extensively, and by the 16th century had leased most of the land to farmers. After the Reformation the monks' land was sold to the Hamilton family.

In 1739 Andrew Buchanan purchased the Drumpellier Estate from the Colquhoun family of Langloan, and in 1741 built Drumpellier House, a Georgian mansion, which was demolished in the late 1960s. The park soon became popular with the townspeople of Coatbridge. During the 1920s and '30s large groups of people from Glasgow arrived by tram and spent their weekends camping by the lochs. In 1984 Drumpellier was officially designated as a Country Park and a visitor centre was opened by the then Provost Cairns of Monkland District Council . Nowadays the park is

popular with passers-by and day-trippers from all over, who arrive by car to take part in the most popular activity by far, feeding the multitude of swans, geese and other birds – or just sitting and watching them.

The handwriting on Willie's entry of birth makes it almost impossible to decipher some of the wording, in particular the street on which he was born. Registrars, even today, have a knack of being totally illegible, yet at the same time very neat. I defy even a doctor to achieve such a dizzy height. I decided to employ the services of Jan Harrison, a handwriting analyst, whom I had known through my work at the BBC. Although this wasn't really her field of expertise, she was kind enough to indulge me and at least have a go at 'translation'. After a few days she called by to see me at the BBC's offices in Northampton to explain that she was reasonably convinced that it read '1 Alexander Street'. Now, I must confess, at first I couldn't see it, but then the individual letters began to make sense. Therefore I decided that, until it could be proven otherwise, it would be fair to assume that this was indeed the place of William's birth.

It seems to me that William must have been named after his great grandfather William Dick.

The Iron Burgh by Alistair Ewen

Coatbridge was famed as the 'Iron Burgh'. The 19th-century boom in iron was made possible by David Mushet's (1801) discovery of blackband ironstone in the bed of North Calder Water and James Beaumont Neilson's invention of the hot blast furnace in 1828. These breakthroughs, together with the ample supply of coal and the benefit of the Monkland Canal for transport, led to a rapid industrialisation of the area from 1830 onwards. By the 1860s there were eight ironworks producing pig-iron from banks of large blast furnaces, and 12 malleable ironworks producing iron rails and plate for

engineering firms in Airdrie and Glasgow. This rapid industrialisation was mirrored by a dramatic increase in population. In the 20 years from 1831 to 1851 the population nearly tripled from 10,000 to just fewer than 30,000. The pressure on housing and living conditions became particularly acute during these years. Over time local supplies of coal and ironstone ran out and new technology made steel cheaper to produce. By the 1920s most of the ironworks had either closed down or switched to rolling steel or tube making. Today only one rolling mill and one tube works remain.

Where the Duncan part of his name came from remains a mystery.

I had the pleasure of meeting two of William's brothers. Great Uncle Gilbert and Aunt Mary were one of the grander aspects of my childhood, and their impending arrival would be heralded by a display of my mother's finest china and instructions to those wearing their Sunday best to be seen and not heard.

In due course their big, bulbous, shiny beautiful Rover car would glide to a stop next to the kerb outside our home. Uncle Gilbert and Aunt Mary would emerge immaculately dressed – always immaculately dressed – with the smell of leather and fine perfumes. It was during one of these visits that I noticed for the first time the 'Nimmo chin'. Many of the Nimmo men inherited a prominent lower jaw, and Uncle Gilbert was no exception – he had a beauty! Children are naturally observant and I had been warned, without reservation, that if I were ever to make mention of the facial characteristic of my mother's Uncle Gilbert then the swift arm of mother law would descend upon my backside with Exocet precision and effect.

It wasn't until 1973, in Vancouver, Canada, that I met the other great Nimmo brother, Thomas Grainger Marshall Nimmo. Again, what a chin and what a gentleman! I'm sure that the somewhat faded picture of Willie that I have displays the same family trait, though perhaps less so than Gilbert and Tom. In addition, from what I have been told, the other brother, my grandfather John, was no exception, although I never had the pleasure of his company – he died long before I was even a twinkle. There were no chinless men in the Nimmo clan!

Great Uncle Tom had also moved to Canada with his wife Nettie and son John Charmichael. I had known and loved John, almost as a brother. Above their fireplace in Vancouver used to be the Nimmo family coat of arms, together with examples of the tartan. I had first met with Uncle Tom and John in 1973 following years of saving for the trip. Indeed, this was the first time that I had been abroad, let alone flown. I fell in love with Vancouver from the word 'go'. Uncle Tom was full of tales about emigrating, helped by the assisted passage programme from the UK in the 'old days' – a sea voyage costing just £10 each. There were so many family members that I had never met or heard of before. It was a magical experience. I was 17 years old and would walk for miles just absorbing this new world – where one still had to 'book' a telephone call home – with the smell of the ocean and the vastness of the Rockies. From that time I always planned, one day, to make Canada my home. I would have to wait a *very* long time.

Today my great-grandparents' home in Church Street has gone. The street still rises up from the drag of the main shopping areas and surrounding ring-road of Coatbridge, but No 58 has long since been demolished and replaced with a 'newer' semi-detached 1960s-looking 58. This 'up-and-over' street is dominated by the terracotta coloured stone of St Andrew's Church, then known as Gartsherrie Church, whose spire can be seen from way outside of the town.

Despite the Nimmo family having been part of the Church Street community for many years, there is no obvious grave headstone in the grounds of St Andrew's that would indicate any burial there of my great-grandparents. However, that is not to say that they are not buried there; I was told that due to extensive vandalism many of the gravestones had been badly defaced, broken or removed. Because of this sad desecration the gates of the church are only unlocked during services. The church itself now represents three churches because of dwindling congregations in two others, which have since been sold off for development. A sign of the times perhaps, indicative of moral decline in a modern world.

2
Royal Edward:
'Fastest to Canada'

Sometimes it feels as if the civilised world was built on Clydeside. Trains, great ships and even the steel that formed them was all produced by Scotsmen, men like my grandfather, who worked in the Glasgow steel industry. It's sometimes difficult to imagine generations of one's own family all living and working for years in a given area, town or street.

My mother, Isabella Watson Marshall Nimmo, was born in Gourock's Bath Street in 1922, and on Thursday 12 June 2003 I arrived at Glasgow's Prestwick airport and drove along the coast road that led to Gourock. The whole region sits in an area of natural beauty with waves crashing in on the road as one makes ones way along the coastal route. My mother's birthplace sits high on a hill facing the Firth, yet tucked away to the side of the main street and shopping areas – blink and you'll miss it. The street itself is a rather sad affair, being a mixture of modern red-brick buildings, 1960s boxy, grey semis and dirty traditional 'granite' black tenement-style homes. A passer-by told me that my grandparents' old home had been demolished to make way for these nondescript drab buildings.

Another chap told me that his family used to run the bakers in Bath Street from premises built in 1920. Dominating the whole of the Bath Street community is St John's Church. My mother and her family would have grown up living next to this church, which leaves its shadow the full length of the street.

I found it ironic that on the day I had chosen to visit the place where my mother was born and had played as a child, her favourite actor, Gregory Peck, had died at the age of 87 in Hollywood. Mum was

Bath Street, Gourock, in 2003, still overlooking the Firth of Clyde. *Author*

never an emotional woman, but this news would have saddened her.

Every new vessel built at the Clydeside shipyards would have passed through the Firth of Clyde and on to the open sea, and there is little doubt that my mother's family would have been quite accustomed to the comings and goings of the Clyde's – and the world's – finest shipping, their pride and joy. So it was that I found myself standing in this street looking out at the Firth and imagining the newly launched *Cairo* of the Egyptian Mail Steamship Company floating by all those years ago on her maiden voyage.

* * *

In the early part of the 20th century any form of travel over a distance was a serious business. Intercontinental travel was especially so, involving vast amounts of preparation. It is worth remembering that those who might travel for pleasure would invariably fall into the category of either First or perhaps Second Class passengers. These would be 'money' people who may also have travelled overseas for the purpose of business – First Class business. The bowels of a steamer would be home to travellers with no less conviction, but with little money or social standing. Third Class, or steerage, passengers were working-class people dreaming of a better life, a new life, in a New World. All travel overseas was a serious business.

This was the era of the fantastic iron-built ocean-going steam liners. In 1907, the year that the *Cairo*, later the *Royal Edward*, was launched, the maiden voyage of the Cunard Line's *Lusitania* had taken place. At 31,500 tons and 790 feet long, she was easily the largest liner in existence at that time, burning some 1,000 tons of coal each and every day.

That same year Pablo Picasso completed *Les Demoiselles d'Avignon* and Claude Monet saw the paint dry on *The Water Lilies*. George Bernard Shaw wrote *The Man of Destiny*. In music, Edward Elgar produced his amazing *Pomp and Circumstance March No 4*, while Jean Sibelius saw his Third Symphony performed for the first time. On board the great steamers that plied the Atlantic routes in that year, the popular tune on every whistler's lips would have been *On The Road To Mandalay*, written by Oley Spears.

The SS *Cairo* was built at yard 450 of shipbuilders Fairfield & Co on the River Clyde, and launched in July 1907. Willie was 17 years old and, hailing from Coatbridge, would undoubtedly have been familiar with the shipyards; he may even have seen the *Cairo* being launched.

Although not the oldest of the Govan shipyards, Fairfield, later Kvaerner-Govan, was at the forefront of shipbuilding technology. It was at this yard that the pupils of Napier, Elder and Pearce helped to make the River Clyde and the term 'Clyde-built' renowned the world over for excellence and durability.

In 1864, John Elder, an engineer, and Charles Randolph, a millwright, had purchased part of Fairfield Farm for the laying out of a new shipyard, and their combined talents established a yard that has been continuously building ships for more than 128 years. Under the company name of Randolph, Elder & Co, ships powered by their newly patented compound steam engine were able to travel greater distances using 30-40% less coal. In 1869 Charles Randolph retired, and John Elder became sole proprietor.

After Elder's untimely death in the same year, Mrs Elder arranged a partnership with her brother, J. F. Ure, J. L. K. Jamieson, and William Pearce, and the name of the company was changed to John Elder & Company, in his memory. In the ensuing years, control of the company came under the sole guidance of William Pearce, who developed new business opportunities with the creation of a new class of transport ships.

The first of these 'Atlantic greyhounds', the SS *Arizona*, won the coveted 'Blue Riband', a prize initiated by William Pearce for the fastest time

Top The *Empress of Canada* being 'finished' at Fairfield. *Author's collection, source unknown*

Above The old Govan 'Fairfield' shipyard in Glasgow, 14 June 2003. Note the demolition of the old Port Authority buildings in the background. *Author*

between Britain and New York. In 1885 Pearce reorganised the yard and renamed it the Fairfield Shipbuilding & Engineering Co Ltd. On his death three years later, control passed to his son, Sir William George Pearce, who led the company to its greatest period of prosperity. He died in 1907, the year that the *Cairo* was launched, and the Northumberland Shipping Co took over until 1935 when Sir John Henry Lithgow for the Lithgow Group acquired the yard. It continued under that company's control until 1965, when the Receivers were called in as Glasgow's biggest shipbuilder faced bankruptcy. The events that followed proved to be a turning point for Clyde shipbuilding, and indeed for British shipbuilding as a whole.

In 1966 the Government intervened and set up a new company, Fairfields, which was backed by the Government, private industry and the Labour Unions. The 'Fairfield Experiment' brought together management and employees in a way hitherto unknown in Clydeside shipbuilding – 'No more Bowlers and Bunnets' (Bowlers representing the management and Bunnets the tradesmen, who had an adversarial relationship). In 1967 the Government proposed amalgamating all of the Upper Clyde Shipyards (Brown, Connel, Stephen, Fairfields and Yarrow) into a group known as the Upper Clyde Shipbuilders, or UCS, but the consortium was doomed to failure. What appeared in theory to be a good solution was in reality unworkable, as each yard specialised in building different kinds of ships. Yarrow withdrew in 1971 and UCS collapsed, going into liquidation. In July of that year the workers staged a 'work-in' that lasted for 14 months, after which a new merger took place and Govan Shipbuilders was born. The yard limped along until 1977, when it was nationalised. In 1988 Kvaerner purchased the yard, bringing in new methods of ship construction and putting the former Fairfield Yard once again at the forefront of shipbuilding technology. In 1999 BAE Systems, the aerospace and defence company formed by the merger of British Aerospace and Marconi Electronic Systems, announced the successful acquisition of the Govan shipyard from Kvaerner. After several months of negotiations, the agreement established Clydeport PLC as landlords of the site, with BAE Systems leasing the land and the buildings for 20 years.

Back in 1907, what a sight the *Cairo* must have been. This shiny new passenger cargo ship was a steel triple-screw steamer weighing in at 11,117 tonnes. She had a length of 545 feet, a beam of 60 feet and a depth of 38 feet. Her keel was about 26 feet below water level. Her coal-fired engines could produce a lot of power compared with other ships at that time. She had 48 furnaces that consumed about 170 tons of coal a day. She had two funnels, two masts, and could run at a top speed of 20 knots; the boilers fed three steam turbines producing 18,000 horsepower. Aboard was accommodation for 344 First, 210 Second and 560 Third class, or steerage, passengers. Her building had been commissioned by the short-lived British-owned Egyptian Mail Steamship Company, together with her sister ship the *Heliopolis*, to serve what was obviously perceived at the time to be the lucrative Marseilles to Alexandria run.

However, someone, somewhere, had seriously miscalculated the profitability of this rather exotic Mediterranean service, and after only a short time the two sisters found themselves laid-up in Marseilles, and in 1909 both were offered for sale. It was a matter of basic economics that it made no sense to have huge amounts of money tied up in this way. Ships cost money. Ships doing nothing cost money. Two ships doing nothing cost a great deal of money, and something had to be done.

Eventually, in 1910, a company called Canadian Northern Steamships, owned by the Canadian Northern Railway Company and commonly known as the 'Royal Line' because of their ships' names, bought both cruisers (probably for a knock-down price).

The Canadian Northern Railway had been incorporated in 1899, following the amalgamation of two small Manitoba grain-transporting branch lines, and was built up over the next 20 years by its principal promoters, William Mackenzie and Donald Mann, to become a 16,093km transcontinental railway with lines connecting Montreal with Vancouver. The company's President, McKenzie was an astute gentleman, keen on efficiency, not too easy to satisfy, and universally feared. On one occasion, the captain of one of the company's ships had a little contretemps with him when he was taking passage to Avonmouth from Montreal. The custom was for the ships to leave Montreal in the early hours of the morning, arriving at Quebec about 2pm, with the sailing time from there fixed for 4.30pm, after loading express packages, the Quebec passengers and the mail, which came by train. On this occasion the ship arrived early, entailing a stop of three hours at Quebec. After reporting as a matter of courtesy to Sir Robert Borden, the Prime Minister of Canada, who was also taking passage in the ship, that the time of departure was 4.30pm, the captain went along to Mackenzie's suite to give him the same information.

Mackenzie had two friends with him, and, instead of accepting the information, opened a discussion on the needless delay at Quebec and the time taken coming down river. It was pointed out that this gave the passengers an opportunity of seeing Quebec, and in any case the sailing schedule was fixed by the Toronto office. The company President was obviously in an argumentative mood, and ended by saying, 'So, we sail at 4.30,' in a manner that indicated, 'See that you're on time.' The captain replied that they would sail at 4.30 – provided that the mail train was on time (this was the first occasion on which the mail had come on the Canadian Northern Quebec Railway, the company's own line). It was then that the captain realised that he had thus dropped a brick.

However, the train was on time, as everyone had been warned to be on top form. As the gangways were raised the captain looked at his watch – it was exactly 4.30. It was then that he saw Sir William checking up on the operation and the time. He learned afterwards that Mackenzie took the first opportunity of putting new officials through a test to size them up.

His partner, Sir Donald Mann, then First Vice-President, was a different type. He was a heavy man, over 6 feet in height. It was said of him that once, when on a business trip to Russia, he had made some remark (probably due to misinterpretation) that offended a Russian Army officer, who challenged him to a duel, offering him a choice of weapons. Sir Donald told his friends that he knew nothing about duelling and would not take part. He was told that this would not do, as he would lose all respect. He thought for a moment, then said, 'Very well, I choose broad-axes.' He had been a pioneer in Canada and was an expert. This was unheard of, but he stuck to his choice, and as a consequence the duel did not take place.

Called 'Canada's Second Transcontinental', the Canadian Northern Railway system was more assembled by connecting small regional railway lines than through the construction of a line across Canada. In 1896 Mackenzie and Mann had acquired the charter of the Lake Manitoba Railway & Canal Company. The first line built by the Canadian Northern under this charter was from Gladstone to Lake Winnipegosis by way of Dauphin. They then obtained running rights southwards from Gladstone to Portage-la-Prairie over the Manitoba & Northwestern Railway. Operations began in 1897, with the name 'Canadian Northern' being adopted two years later. Mackenzie and Mann then turned their attention to the east, and began construction of the Manitoba & Southeastern Railway. This line ran initially from St Boniface (across the Red River from Winnipeg) to Marchand. This 45-mile line, opened in 1898, paid its way by hauling firewood to Winnipeg. Further construction of the Manitoba & Southeastern, combined with the acquisition of short lines, permitted the Canadian Northern to reach Port Arthur (now Thunder Bay), Ontario, in 1902.

By 1905 a line had been completed between Winnipeg and Edmonton. In 1908, surveys of the Rocky Mountains were undertaken, but the situation became critical with the onset of war in Europe in 1914, when financial markets essentially became frozen. It was nonetheless decided to build a line through Yellowhead Pass, and to follow the Fraser River to Vancouver; a line completed in 1915. During this period the railway completed construction of the Lake Superior gap between Port Arthur and Ottawa via Capreol, while also building a line between Toronto and Sudbury.

Freight services between Toronto and Winnipeg started in 1915 and, later, passenger service between Quebec and Vancouver. A new passenger terminal was built in Montreal, requiring the construction of a 3-mile tunnel beneath Mount Royal to access it.

The Canadian Northern Railway had been built as inexpensively as possible, with plans to make improvements to the later line as passenger and freight traffic developed. However, the railway was taken over by the Canadian Government in 1918 after a period of financial difficulty.

Meanwhile, under Canadian Northern ownership, the *Cairo* and *Heliopolis* would never be the same again. They both underwent alteration: the topmost deck of each ship was removed, and the hull greatly strengthened for Atlantic weather. The liners were luxuriously furnished, and equipped with all the conveniences of a modern floating hotel. To mention only one feature, communication between the four passenger decks was provided by electric lift. Both ships were fitted with wireless and 'submarine signalling apparatus'. However, before they were ready to embark on their new life, their owners insisted on changing their names. Something royal. Something regal.

Now, you may call me superstitious but I was always led to believe that it was tempting fate to change the names of horses, houses and ships. I don't know why, and I don't know where the idea came from – it's just one of those useless pieces of uselessness that one carries around in one's head. Nevertheless, the *Heliopolis* was re-christened the *Royal George* – in honour of the reigning monarch King George V – and the *Cairo* became the *Royal Edward*, in honour of the late King Edward VII. Their new home port was now Toronto in Canada.

During its time on the Atlantic service, the *Royal Edward* carried many distinguished English and Canadian statesmen to and fro, including Earl

Below **An artist's impression of the RMS *Royal Edward* under full steam. This picture, printed and published by C. W. Hunt & Co of Liverpool, was used to illustrate postcards sent by passengers from the ship.** *Author's collection*

Opposite **'Fastest to Canada': the *Royal Edward* (*above*) and the *Royal George*.** *Author's collection/GWPDA*

CUNARD R.M.S. ROYAL GEORGE AT AVONMOUTH, BRISTOL.

Above A painting by Dalmonte of the Café-Lounge on the RMS *Royal Edward. GWPDA*

Below The dining salon on board the *Royal Edward. GWPDA*

The *Royal Edward*'s very 'POSH' library. *GWPDA*

Grey, Governor-General of Canada, and Sir Robert Laird Borden, who became the eighth Canadian Premier. A large traffic was also done with emigrants between Bristol and Canada, the West of England being the favourite area for Canadian emigration agents before the Great War. Details of Canadian immigration can be found in the Government of Canada Sessional Papers, Government Immigration Reports, and passenger list records. In the early years the report for the port of Quebec was the only one given. Later, reports sometimes appeared for Halifax, St John, New Brunswick and a few other places such as Hamilton. Other ports marked in records are Portland, Maine, North Sydney, and St John's, Newfoundland.

The numbers given in the various categories changed their meaning over the years. For example, at one time a male was any male over 12 years, a female any female over 12 years, and a child was over one year of age and an infant under one. Sometimes all children of 12 and under were listed as 'child' and the infant category was not used.

The numbers of passengers given did not always agree with the numbers that were quoted in other Government reports. Dates were also not consistent, sometimes being given and sometimes not. Later, forms changed so that ships' names were not given but the destination of the party was. It all seemed somewhat haphazard.

Most available information was for all 'assisted' passages, that is *all* the organisations bringing children as well as reformatories, industrial schools and emigration groups, such as the East End Emigration Society and the Clerkenwell Emigration Committee. These latter two groups, and others like them, brought hundreds of families and adults to Canada.

Some examples of those that arrived in Canada on board the *Royal Edward* are as follows:

On 25 September 1912 the *Royal Edward* arrived in Canada carrying a 'Miss Joyce party' of 'domestics' and a 'Miss Lightbourne party' of 'domestics'. 'Miss Rothwell's party' of 'domestics' also arrived that day.

On 7 May 1913 another group, listed this time as 'Mrs' Joyce party, arrived, and a further group of 'Miss Lightbourne party' of 'domestics' arrived.

On 8 July 1913, Mrs Joyce party, British Women's Emigration Association (domestics), Hone & Rivet party (families), Miss Lightbourne party (domestics), the Abbot party and the Roth party are all listed as arriving in Canada aboard the *Royal Edward*.

The North Atlantic was, and still is on occasion, a very inhospitable place to be in any sized vessel. First Class passengers on the *Royal Edward* were generally what one might describe as 'POSH'. Many would have described the ship itself as being very POSH. Indeed, the very word POSH may have been created in the North Atlantic, with the instruction being given for passengers to stay Portside Outbound from Avonmouth, as a protection from the northerly wind, and from Canada to England the instruction would be Starboard Home, again for protection from the north winds.

Some say that 'POSH' was the legend printed on tickets of passengers on P&O (Peninsular & Orient) passenger vessels when travelling between Britain and India in the days of the Raj. Britain and India are both in the Northern Hemisphere so the port (left-hand-side) berths were mostly in the shade when travelling out (eastwards) and the starboard ones when coming back. So the best and most expensive berths were POSH, hence the term. It's a very plausible and attractive explanation, but this does appear to be an idea that was dreamed up retrospectively to match an existing meaning. P&O says that it has never issued such tickets, and although many tickets from that era still exist, no 'POSH' ones have been found. Numerous letters and literary works also

remain from the British Raj, but nothing has been found to confirm the word being used in that context. The word doesn't seem to have been used in print before a *Punch* cartoon dated 1918, although it was used from the mid-19th century to mean a 'dandy', which is the more likely derivation of the current meaning.

The most detailed and colourful account of the acronym is a letter from a retired mariner who recalled in considerable detail (including the violet letters) how in 1913 he had seen such a P&O round-trip ticket in the possession of a man returning to Hong Kong. He had missed his P&O ship in Italy and was thus a passenger on the same ship (of a different steamship line) as the letter-writer. This man, a European official employed by the Chinese Government, had booked his trip in Hong Kong and was thus making the round-trip in a direction opposite to that of the English gentry on their way to the Raj. According to the theory, his ticket should have been stamped 'SOPH' to assure him cool accommodation – but the writer recalls a violet 'POSH'.

However, I still quite like to believe in the North Atlantic theory – it's the romantic in me. To think of all of those POSH people walking the decks of the *Royal Edward*, known for her rolling motion, in the middle of a chilly Atlantic night, while the engines were being kept in tip-top condition by the likes of Willie and his 'comrades', working away far below decks – and far from POSH!

For some reason, and despite the lack of information in the public domain, emigration details from Europe to Canada seem to focus on specific groups of people. As an example, here are four departures and arrivals of Germans from Russia arriving in Quebec aboard the RMS *Royal Edward* from 1910 until the outbreak of war in 1914. These were the last of their kind, escaping what was to become the main theatre of hostilities.

Depart: Bristol, 29 September 1910. Arrive: Quebec, 6 October 1910.

Joseph Miller, 50, headed for Calgary accompanied by Felisantha, 49, Friedrich, 18, Karl, 10, Anna, 20, Emilia, 8, and Petrak Wilhelm, 20.

Below **A rare postcard of 'The arrival of the** *Royal Edward* **at New Passenger Station, Avonmouth Dock, April 29th 1910' prior to her maiden voyage to Canada.** *Author's collection, source unknown*

Bottom **RMS** *Royal Edward* **moored at Avonmouth.** *Author's collection*

Depart: Bristol, 31 May, 1911. Arrive: Quebec, 7 June 1911.

Conrad Hohnstein, 48, headed for Stoney Plain in Alberta, accompanied by Anna, 46, Johann, 16, Heinrich, 14, Lisa, 11, Maria, 8, and Conrad Junior, 4.

Depart: Avonmouth, 29 May 1912. Arrive: Quebec, 8 June 1912.

Jacob Schtell, 26, headed for Stoney Plain, Alberta, accompanied by Katherine, aged 20.

The Arrival of the Royal Edward at New Passenger Station, Avonmouth Dock, April 29th 1910.

Left A postcard view of the *Royal Edward* entering Avonmouth. *Author's collection*

Below left The *Royal Edward* moored at shed 'P', Avonmouth docks. *Author's collection, source unknown*

Right A *Royal Edward* passenger postcard posted from Quebec to Bristol on 7 May 1913: 'Dear Lizzie, Arrived safe. Bad all day on Thursday but in the pink now. Love to all from Mill.' *Author's collection*

Below left The *Royal Edward* being 'serviced' at Avonmouth. *Author's collection, source unknown*

Depart: Avonmouth, 26 July 1913. Arrive: Quebec, 3 August, 1913.
Elizabeth Schalz, 31, headed for Toronto, accompanied by Franz, 23, and Gustav, 19.

To this day there are some Canadians and Americans who believe that their ancestors arrived on the *Royal Edward* after embarking at some port in Cornwall. This was never the case.

The one outstanding feature of the commercial economy of Great Britain during the second half of the 19th century was the uninterrupted development of South Wales as the greatest steam-coal-exporting centre in the country. The 1919 Royal Commission on the Coal Industry came to

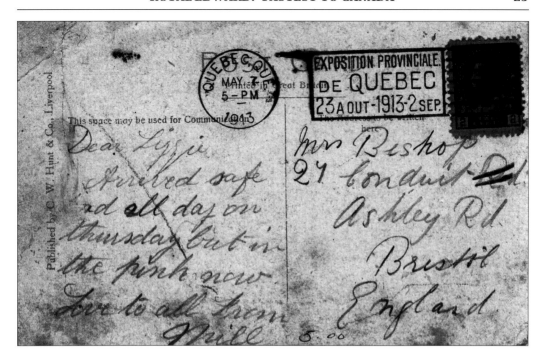

the conclusion that the prosperity of South Wales and Monmouthshire 'is entirely dependant on the export trade in coal.' Ships needed coal – a great deal of coal!

In the field of the Merchant Marine, Cymmer coal from collieries owned by Insoles was in constant demand by the Peninsular & Orient Steam Navigation Company, the Compagnie Generale Transatlantique, the White Star Line, Messageries de France, and Austrian Lloyd's Steam Navigation Co Ltd. The following steamship companies were supplied by the Lewis Merthyr Consolidated Collieries Co Ltd: Cunard, White Star, Pacific & Oriental, Union Castle, Hansa, Anchor, Adria, Royal Hungarian Sea Navigation, and Generale-Transatlantique. Increased prestige was gained by the part that Rhondda steam coal played in the winning of the Blue Riband by the *Mauritania* powered by Ocean steam coal, and the fastest passage from Bristol to Quebec by the *Royal Edward*, powered by Ferndale steam coal.

The 'Royals' were perhaps the first liners to take bunker coal in Montreal through side ports, and

consequently there were no facilities for doing this. Previously they had used lighters on the off side, and coal from carts that was dumped on the quay and had to be shovelled in from the shore side, resulting in slow and expensive work, apart from the coal dust permeating the cargo shed even when the passengers were embarking. To overcome this it was proposed to 'boom' the ships off from the wooden pier, and bringing lighters also on the inside, as was the practice of most of the liner companies in New York. However, conditions were entirely different on the pier at Montreal. There were no steam winches or other power-source on the pier to boom the ships off, and the Port Warden informed the captains of the Royal Line that ships lay within 50 feet of their sterns beyond the end of the pier.

This was discouraging to the captains of both the *Royal Edward* and the *Royal George*, but after consideration they felt that the responsibility must be accepted in order to improve the bunkering arrangements. After making representation to the Harbour Commissioners, instructions were issued

One of the 'Royals' coaling through side ports at
St John, New Brunswick, in the winter of 1913-14.
F. J. Thompson

by them that all ships were to reduce speed to a minimum on passing the Canadian Northern Railway Pier. In making the contract for bunker coal it was stipulated that the contractor should provide lighters with winches and with stump derrick posts to go under the booms, between the ship and the pier.

The usual method of booming liners off from the dockside was to place one end of the boom on a pad on the ship's side at right angles to the ship, one forward, another aft. Tackles were then rigged from eye-bolts at the dockside to the heel of the booms, which led to a winch or winches and the ships were hove off as the moorings were slackened. As there was no power on the Montreal pier, the crews had to adopt an alternative method. The booms were landed on the ship's rail (overhanging across the width of the ship), the dock ends were secured to the pier, and tackles rigged from the ship end to the bulwark stanchions and leading to winches. On heaving away and easing the moorings the ship hove herself off from the pier under her own power.

On arrival of the first ship (the *Royal George*, which was also first to enter the St Lawrence that year, in April 1911), the captain was the recipient of the traditional gold-headed cane from the Harbour Commissioners. It was an anxious moment when they came to boom off for the first time, but all went well and though the ships ranged a little when other vessels passed, they had additional springs out and no casualty occurred throughout the season. Three days completed the bunkering of some 1,800 tons of coal instead of the usual six days, which had previously meant coaling up to the last hour before sailing.

The captains reported that it was satisfactory and interesting work in Montreal as they had almost a free hand. Under Canadian railway organisation the superintendent was the operating official, the agents obtaining the passengers and cargo. The marine superintendent was thereby in charge of the operation of the steamships and reported when necessary to the head office in Toronto. Both captains made frequent visits to

Toronto between sailings, travelling by Pullman sleeper one night and returning the next.

It was during this period of service in Montreal that, in order to stimulate interest in lifeboat drill, a series of lifeboat races was inaugurated between the different departments of the ships, with boats manned by seamen, firemen and stewards. Two lifeboats were kept in the water for the purpose of training crews. On the first occasion a monetary prize was provided by subscription from the captain and officers, but later other sources were tapped. The races took place between Windmill Point and the stern of the ships, off King Edward Pier, while the harbour authorities kindly provided a launch or tug to supervise. The Montreal newspapers gave publicity to the events, and after the first race a considerable number of spectators gathered.

When the subject was raised by the Second Vice-President during the captains' next visit to Toronto, they explained that the idea was to stimulate interest in lifeboat drill and to improve the boat-craft of the men. At the same time they asked for a donation for prizes and suggested a challenge shield, which was duly forthcoming. The winning crews had their names engraved on the shield, which was placed in each ship in a conspicuous position on the main staircase and proved of considerable interest to passengers. The men grew keen, and while the stewards provided themselves with blue singlets the seamen adopted white and the firemen red.

In one of the ships the firemen's crew invariably won, and while it was appreciated that their back muscles were well developed through shovelling coal, the question was asked of the chief engineer how he accounted for it. He replied to the effect that the stroke oar of the firemen's boat was formerly coxswain to 'Jackie Fisher' (Admiral of the Fleet Lord Fisher) when the latter was a captain and that this former bluejacket coached the boat's crew. There was a certain amount of cynicism on the waterfront about this 'craze for lifeboat pulling', but criticism ceased the following year after the *Titanic* disaster.

The captain of the *Royal George*, F. J. Thompson, reported at that time that he liked Halifax, where he had several close friends, and that, except for the trouble of changing homes and missing the prospect of the winter sports in Montreal, it made an agreeable change. The passenger traffic was not so heavy but he says he also had the intermediate ships from Rotterdam *(Uranium, Campanello* and *Volturno)* to look after as the Royal Line now had its own office.

April 1912 was a sad month, the *Titanic* disaster throwing a gloom over the town for some time. All the bodies that were recovered from the sea were landed at Halifax, Nova Scotia, for burial. On the actual night of the tragedy the captain of the *Royal George* was dining at the Halifax Club with Mr Hernsley, and the former captain of HMS *Niobe* was having dinner with a Mr M. Morrow, the representative of the Dominion Coal Company. Before dinner, when the early reports of the collision with an iceberg came in and ships were proceeding to the rescue, they all discussed the situation and in particular the previous unfortunate statement that the ship was unsinkable – a view, incidentally, not held by those who new the power of the deep. After dinner, when playing bridge in the smoking room, Mr Morrow was called to the telephone. On his return to the card table he said, 'I have been through to New York – the *Titanic* has sunk.' It was a dramatic moment. Everyone dropped their cards and there was no more bridge played that night.

Warnings about the danger of ice had been passing from vessel to vessel as they steamed the Atlantic all that day and night. During the Board of Trade enquiry that followed *Titanic*'s demise, the captain of a ship called the *Canada*, of the Dominion line, was called to give evidence. Master Richard O. Jones told the Solicitor General that they had received warnings of ice from the *Royal Edward*, which had reported field ice and bergs at

42° 48'. The exact message had read: 'The *Royal Edward* this morning reports bergs 42-48°N, 49-40°W, and passed through ice-field in 42-35°N and 50-18°W, extending N and S as far as visible. Some of this ice is heavy and dangerous.'

Ocean-going steamships like the *Royal Edward* of the Royal Line were in direct competition with the ships of the Canadian Pacific Railway out of Liverpool. The speed of crossing was a pressure point for captains, who had discretion as to whether to take the northerly, shorter, route, having regard to known ice conditions. The *Titanic* inquiry was to highlight the question of speed and the use of the northerly Atlantic routes.

Following the disaster, the White Star Line, owner of the RMS *Titanic*, chartered two cable-laying steamers, the *Mackay-Bennett* and the *Minia*, to locate and identify bodies. Two days after the sinking, the *Mackay-Bennett* sailed from Halifax and eventually recovered 306 bodies, of which 190 were returned to Halifax. One of the cable engineers on the *Mackay-Bennett*, Frederick Hamilton, kept a diary of the voyage, which makes mention of the *Royal Edward*:

'April 19th

The fine weather which has prevailed until now, has turned to rain and fog. We spoke to the *Royal Edward* by wireless to-day, she lay east of us, and reported icebergs, and growlers [lumps of ice, some of considerable size]. At 6pm the fog very dense, lowered cutter and picked up an Allan Line lifebelt.

April 20th

Strong south-westerly breeze, beam swell and lumpy sea. French liner *Rochambeau* near us last night, reported icebergs, and the *Royal Edward* reported one thirty miles east of the *Titanic*'s position…'

Several days later the *Mackay-Bennett* returned to Halifax.

'April 30th, 8.25am: Took Pilot on board off Devils Island, and are now proceeding up Halifax Harbour. Crowds of people throng the wharves, tops of houses, and the streets. Flags on ships and buildings all half mast. Quarantine and other officials came on board near Georges Island, after which ship stood in to the Navy Yard, and hauled in alongside. Elaborate arrangement have been made for the reception of the bodies now ready for landing. 10am: Transferring of remains to shore has begun. A continuous procession of hearses conveys the bodies to the Mayflower Rink. It is a curious reflection, that when on February 12th, we picked up the waterlogged schooner *Caledonia* and returned to Halifax to land her crew of six, these men walked ashore unnoticed, and two lines in the Daily Paper was sufficient to note the fact that they had been saved. While today, with not one life to show, thousands come to see the landing, and the papers burst out into blazing headlines. On 7th May the *Royal Edward*, en route from Cape Ray to Bird Rocks, steamed for 20 miles through loose field ice. Some things never change…'

During the summer season of 1912 the organisation ran smoothly and the services of the Royal Line became very popular. In 1913 the Royal Line captains had the honour of being elected as Younger Brothers of the Corporation of Trinity House, an ancient body of sea captains, Mercantile and Naval, that dates back to the reign of Henry VII. The Brethren met at the annual Court on Trinity Monday, when ten would elect the Master and Deputy Master and Wardens for the ensuing year, after which they would proceed to a divine service, held at St Olave's Church and subsequently on to luncheon with the Elder Brethren.

On the Wednesday following Trinity Monday the Elder Brethren gave a dinner to the Younger Brethren, always formerly held at Trinity House, destroyed by fire in the blitz of December 1940. The Younger Brethren's dinner was a unique function, the whole assembly, with the single exception of the Bishop who preached on Trinity Monday, composed of captains or former captains of ships, Naval and Mercantile. No guests were allowed.

The two ships once again had a very satisfactory season and made some very good passages, the best of which occurred in July 1913 when a record run of 3 days 19 hours 25 minutes was made by the *Royal Edward* land to land from Belle Isle to the Irish coast, the voyage from Quebec to Avonmouth occupying 5 days 17 hours 4 minutes. The ship docked at Avonmouth at breakfast time, which enabled passengers bound to the Continent to dine that night in Paris less than seven days after leaving Montreal. The *Royal Edward* and the *Royal George*, though not quite so big as the *Empress of Britain* and the *Empress of Ireland* of the Canadian Pacific Railway Company, were a little faster, and certainly their great rivals.

The voyages that year were made more interesting in that the White Star Line had placed the *Teutonic*, its old New York 'crack' liner, on the Canadian route, and she was scheduled to sail from Liverpool on the same day as the *Royal George* from Avonmouth. Both ships also sailed within a few hours of each other from Quebec. Consequently they had some interesting, if unofficial, races, and there was considerable rivalry among the crews. The various captains were good friends and exchanged daily wireless messages, reporting their positions and day's run.

On one occasion, after the *Teutonic* had made a better day's run than the 'Royals', the captain concluded his message with 'have given stokers a tot of rum'. The next day the *Royal George* made a better run and the captain concluded his message with 'have been feeding firemen on cocktails'. They made many interesting competitive voyages, for both ships were nominally at least of the same speed, although both of the 'Royals' were of much later construction. Moreover they often 'split tacks' (took

Left **A view from the mainmast looking toward the stern. Note some of the crew or passengers just visible centre left.** *F. J. Thompson*

Below **One of the 'Royals' butting the waves on one of their numerous Atlantic crossings.** *F. J. Thompson*

An advertisement in the *Literary Digest* on 13 June 1914. The 'Royals' continued to steam across the Atlantic Ocean right up to the declaration of war on 4 August 1914. Indeed, even with the hint of hostility in the air, the Royal Line continued to advertise its transatlantic services. *Author's collection*

The *Royal Edward*'s Gentlemen's Smoking Room (*below*), and the ship's Music Room (*bottom*). *Both GWPDA*

All the comforts of home, and some, were provided to the passengers and senior officers of the *Royal Edward*. Many of us will have seen the modern film based around the final days of the *Titanic* and might be forgiven for thinking that all steerage, or Third Class, passengers lived among the ship's rats and survived on ale, bread and Irish music. Not so. Even these lowly folk were offered a full and varied diet on board the ships of the Royal Line. Looking at the Third Class breakfast menu from the *Royal Edward* dated 18 July 1912, only three months following the sinking of the *Titanic*, it would seem that the cost

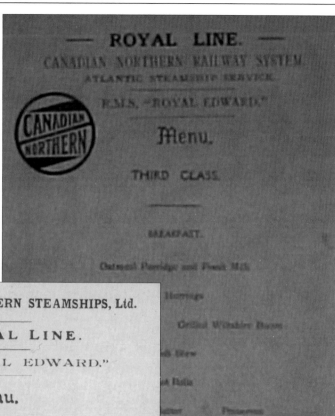

of a Third Class ticket bought one a good start to the day, with a choice of porridge with fresh milk, red herrings (yes, there really is such a thing), fried eggs with grilled Wiltshire bacon, Irish stew, hot rolls, fresh bread and butter, preserves, and rounded off with a choice of either tea or coffee. One can only imagine the grand breakfasts that may have been in store for those lucky enough to be travelling in the upper decks.

Kathryn Atkin/Author's collection, source unknown

alternative routes during the summer), the White Star ship having to follow the company's rule book as to the route she took (via Cape Race or Belle Isle) on a certain date. No such rule applied with the Royal Line, the captain exercising his own judgment in accordance with the ice reports that varied each season. The result was that the modern ship scored over the old-timer. It was then remarked by the *Teutonic* supporters: 'Wait until the winter comes, then the old ship will show the way.'

The captains of the line also made it their job to take an interest in the engine-room and stokeholds of their ships, and made it a practice on a fine day each voyage to visit the engine-room department with the Chief Engineer after the forenoon inspection. It would be on such occasions that they would have a few words of encouragement to say to the leading fireman or other men on watch.

Making record passages across the Atlantic

'Flagship Canadian Northern Steamships Limited. Holds Canadian Atlantic Record 15 Days 20 Hours! Bristol to Quebec.' A postcard recording the *Royal Edward*'s capturing of the Canadian westbound record. The crew of the *Royal George* were desirous of equalling her reputation for speed. *Author's collection, source unknown*

depended on a number of factors, not the least of which was the weather (others were good coal and sound engine-room staff). If the weather was foul with head winds or fog, fast passages could not be made. However, an opportunity came in July of that year when the *Royal George* captured the eastbound Canadian record, having light winds, a smooth sea and overcast sky all the way across. The winter of 1913/14 was a foul one and rather to everyone's chagrin the 'Royals' were ordered (for political reasons, it is believed) to make St John, New Brunswick, their winter port in lieu of Halifax, NS, the Canadian Pacific Railways ships making the latter their terminal port.

The Royal Line carried many prominent and interesting passengers during this period. Among them was the Minister of Militia (Colonel Sam Hughes, afterwards General Sir Sam Hughes) and his Militia party, including several wives crossing to see the 'Army manoeuvres' in England and on the Continent in 1913. On another occasion the Forbes-Robertson party (which had been touring Canada) returned with them and they all had many bright entertainments, concluding with such things as fancy dress dances in the café on the boat deck.

I found just one marriage at sea recorded in the 'Royal Line' archives (see Register of Marriages at Sea in the Public Record Office, ref: BT 334/117). It took place aboard the *Royal George* on 25 July 1914 between a ship's fireman employed by the Grand Trunk Railway, called Francis Mark Randolph Hider (29), and Annie Reeves (28). Annie's father, for the record, was Charles, an engineer, and her new husband's father was a gardener called Mark. The ceremony was performed by a French minister, M La Touche, in the presence of the ship's master Frederick J. Thompson, mentioned earlier just prior to the sinking of the *Titanic* in 1912.

The summer season of 1914 was a good one. The two liners were gaining yet more in popularity, both passenger and cargo traffic was increasing, and a regular schedule was maintained. One dark spot on the Canadian Atlantic service was the tragic loss of the *Empress of Ireland*, which, after collision with the Norwegian cargo vessel *Storstad*, sank in the vicinity of Father Point with great loss of life. Everyone in the Royal Line felt the tragedy very keenly, for they were friendly rivals and no competitive instinct affected the regard and good relations existing among those who went down to the sea in ships.

On the Atlantic there is a great difference in weather conditions proceeding eastward as compared to westward, as barograph records clearly show. When westbound a ship is constantly meeting depressions (except in very settled conditions), whereas when running to the east she may run across in a high-pressure area or between depressions all the way. The Western Ocean holds a great attraction for many seamen, although the voyage, particularly on the Canadian route, is perhaps the hardest regular trade from the UK.

In June 1914 the *Royal Edward* made some of the earliest practical demonstrations in wireless direction finding. She was specially fitted with the Marconi-Belline-Tosi system of direction finding, and one of the Marconi Company's engineers made the voyage in the ship to carry out the tests. These proved very satisfactory and they were able to obtain wireless bearings within 5 degrees of accuracy between 50 and 70 miles. As no other ships were so fitted at that time they had to send a wireless message to a ship within that distance, requesting her to make a succession of Vs to enable the *Royal Edward* to take a bearing. All ships met with ready co-operation, as did the operators at wireless stations in the St Lawrence, beginning with Cape Race. The experiments convinced all at the time of the great aid to navigation that this new invention foretold.

So, for the best part of three and a half years the two passenger steamers, complete with their grand Royal names, serviced the needs of their transatlantic passengers. From May 1910 to September 1914 the *Royal Edward* was used on the Avonmouth-Quebec/Montreal route in the summer and Halifax, Nova Scotia, in the winter, but in the autumn of 1914 all that would change for ever.

3
His Majesty's Transport

By the time that King George V came to the throne in 1910 William Nimmo was 20 years old – from Victorian to Edwardian to Georgian in such a short life. It is not clear when, exactly, he joined the Canadian Mercantile Marine. Indeed, when the *Cairo* became the *Royal Edward*, his contract may well have transferred from British to Canadian automatically.

In 1914 the smell of war was in the air, and during such a conflict the Government would commandeer any craft worth her salt to serve as a troop carrier. In the autumn of that year both the RMS *Royal George* and the RMS *Royal Edward* became troopships in the service of their country. Indeed, the newly styled HMT *Royal Edward*

Canada's Answer by Norman Wilkinson. The original painting, some 215cm x 368cm, is held by the Canadian War Museum in Ottawa. *Princess Royal* has three signal pendants hoisted from her starboard yardarm: '2', '6', then one with a blue cross on a white background. The latter may be a mistake: a red cross on a white background was '3'. Also hoisted, but difficult to make out even on the original, is the red flag flapping directly in line with the mast: that is the Canadian Red Ensign. *GWPDA*

assisted in bringing the Canadian troop contingent to England. Overnight they had been transformed from Royal Mail Steamers to His Majesty's Transports.

So, William was in the Canadian Mercantile Marine when the Great War began. Very little is known of his life, yet I feel safe to assume that Willie was, by then, already in Canada working for the 'Royal Line'. He would have been on either the *Royal George* or the *Royal Edward*, preparing to carry Canadian troops and goods to the European theatre of war. Canada was part of the British Empire and was not backward in coming forward to repel the Kaiser's threat.

The following details are extracted from the article *Troop Convoy – How Canada Went to War in 1914*, in *Crowsnest*, November 1964 (the Christmas issue), which in turn summarised the speech given by Rear-Admiral Hugh Pullen RCN on 10 October 1964 to the Red Chevron Club of Ottawa (whose members were those who had gone overseas with the First Contingent – 32,000 men – of the Canadian Expeditionary Force in October 1914).

Arrangements for the transportation of the First Contingent were started on 15 August 1914 when the Minister of Militia, Sir Sam Hughes – no stranger to the Royal Line – held a meeting with the representatives of the larger shipping companies. Ships were needed to carry some 25,000 men across the North Atlantic, sailing about the middle of September. Contracts were signed by 11 September for 20 ships, increased to 30 when it was decided to send the entire force that had been assembled at Valcartier. The merchant ships were prepared for their troopship role at Montreal, and as soon as they were ready they proceeded down the river to Quebec to embark their troops.

The embarkation of men, horses, guns, stores and equipment at Quebec was carried out with difficulty. A plan had been drawn up, but it was discarded due to delays in the arrival of the troopships and changes in the number to be embarked, to say nothing of the interference of the Minister of Militia. As one officer described it, 'chaos reigned supreme'. I do not think one should be overly critical when it is remembered that an unmilitary nation had raised a force of nearly 30,000 fighting men in about six weeks, and was sending it overseas. Many lessons were learned by many people concerned with the movement of fighting men across the sea, and on the whole they were not forgotten in 1939.

Only three ships were loaded according to the plan drawn up by the Director of Supplies and Transport. Then the Minister interfered, and the plan collapsed.

Embarkation began on 23 September 1914, when the mounted units marched to Quebec. The infantry went by rail. The last ship was loaded and sailed on Thursday 1 October at 5pm. In a few cases a single unit, complete in all respects, was on board the same ship. One unit had to disembark due to lack of accommodation; some ships had to load ballast to give them stability, and in the end an extra ship had to be found to embark the men, horses and stores that had been left behind.

The total figures for the First Contingent are well worth remembering: 1,547 officers; 29,070 men; 7,679 horses; 70 guns; 110 motor vehicles; 705 horse-drawn vehicles; and 82 bicycles This was a most impressive force for any small nation to raise in less than two months, and may be the largest fleet ever to put to sea. The troops and merchant seamen were all volunteers and worthy representatives of Canada. As each ship was loaded, she went out into the river and anchored. There the Master was given his sealed orders. The first directed him to proceed down the river. The second, to be opened after the pilot had been dropped at Father Point, instructed him to proceed to an anchorage in Gaspé Bay, which would be given to him by CGS *Canada*, carrying out a patrol off the entrance to the bay. The third was a message from the Governor General, HRH the Duke of Connaught, which was to be read to the troops:

'On the eve of your departure from Canada I wish to congratulate you on having the privilege of taking part, with the other forces of the Crown, in fighting for the Honour of the King and Empire.

You have nobly responded to the call of duty, and Canada will know how to appreciate the patriotic spirit that animates you.

I have complete confidence that you will do your duty, and that Canada will have every reason to be proud of you.

You leave these shores with the knowledge that all Canadian hearts beat for you, and that our prayers and best wishes will ever attend you.

May God bless you and bring you back victorious.

ARTHUR, FM
Governor General of Canada'

The Minister had asked the Department of Marine and Fisheries and the Department of the Naval Service 'to make sure that every possible precaution be taken to detect and prevent the laying of mines in the river or on the route to England.' As there was no minesweeping gear of any sort, this request was quite impractical. All that could be done was to keep a good lookout.

When the 30 transports reached their anchorages in Gaspé Bay safely, they were ordered to be darkened at night and silence was to be observed. Some form of security was instituted, but in general, as it affected the sailing of the First Contingent, it was not good.

On joining the convoy off Cape Race, the *Florizel*, with the Newfoundland Contingent on board, took station astern of the *Cassandra*. The *Manhattan*, which had the 'stragglers', proceeded independently.

The Minister had been greatly concerned about the safety of the convoy, but was reassured when the Admiralty informed him that the escort would consist of four cruisers, HMCS *Niobe*, and a battleship, HMS *Glory*. A second battleship would join during the passage across the Atlantic.

Rear-Admiral Phipps-Hornby was in command of the North American Squadron with his flag in the battleship HMS *Glory*. The other ships in the Squadron were HMS *Suffolk*, *Essex* and *Lancaster*, *Caronia* (AMC) and HMCS *Niobe*. Rear-Admiral Wemyss, in command of the 12th Cruiser Squadron – HMS *Charybdis* (flag), *Talbot*, *Eclipse* and *Diana* – was ordered to act as escort for the troop convoy. Wemyss arrived at Halifax with three of his ships on 22 September, while the *Diana*, which had been delayed with defects, reached Sydney on the 23rd. Rear-Admiral Phipps-Hornby was ordered to shift his flag to the *Lancaster*, and put the *Glory* and *Niobe* under Rear-Admiral Wemyss's command. HMS *Majestic* from the 7th Battle Squadron was ordered to reinforce the escort. It was thought that if the convoy was attacked it would probably be during the second half of the voyage; in case this did happen, the C-in-C Home

Fleet was ordered to send either HMS *Queen Mary* or *Princess Royal* (battle cruisers) to the rendezvous and to be there by 2 October. The *Princess Royal* was detailed, and stayed with the convoy until she reached the Fastnet, off southern Ireland.

Rear-Admiral Phipps-Hornby pointed out that his squadron would be too weak to keep a proper watch on the German ships known to be in US ports, so *Niobe* was returned to him. On arrival at Halifax, Rear-Admiral Wemyss went up to Quebec to discuss the arrangements for the convoy with the Minister. He asked that the rendezvous at Gaspé Bay and the time of sailing be kept secret. The inhabitants of the area were most co-operative and the secret was well kept.

Wemyss sailed with his squadron from Halifax on 26 September and the whole squadron arrived at Gaspé & Eactue Bay on the 28th. The troopships arrived in batches, three on 29 September, 13 on 1

October, 12 on 2 October, and two during that night. The Minister visited the anchorage on the 2nd, and distributed copies of his farewell message to the troops. After seeing only four cruisers he became greatly concerned once more about the strength of the escort – he was of the opinion that it was quite inadequate, and said so.

Finally the Admiralty replied that, 'My Lords are satisfied that every reasonable precaution has been taken and the escort is considered safe… The cancelling of the sailing on the ground of inadequate escort will rest, therefore, with the Canadian Government.'

However, the Admiralty told no one about the plan to support the convoy with a battlecruiser during the second half of the voyage. It seems incredible that they did not tell Rear-Admiral Wemyss, who was responsible for the safety of the convoy.

List of the ships in the convoy of 3 October 1914, in random order (ie not in the order in which they lined up for sailing)

From Colonel A. Fortesque Duguid's *Official History of the Canadian Forces in the Great War* (King's Printer, Ottawa, 1938)

1st Canadian Division,
Canadian Expeditionary Force

Warships

HM Ship	Type
Charybdis	Old cruiser (Astraea Class)
Diana	Old cruiser (Eclipse Class)
Eclipse	Old cruiser (Eclipse Class)
Talbot	Old cruiser (Eclipse Class)
Glory	Pre-Dreadnought (Canopus Class)
Magnificent	Pre-Dreadnought (Majestic Class)
Princess Royal	Battlecruiser (Lion Class)

Transports

(The breakdown by column within the convoy is taken from *Troop Convoy – How Canada Went to War in 1914*, in *Crowsnest*, October 1964. The article notes that as the troopships arrived in Gaspé Bay they were anchored in the positions they would hold in the convoy on sailing. They were in three columns, Z, Y, and X.)

Z (Blue Squadron)	Y (White Squadron)	X (Red Squadron)
Megantic	*Royal Edward*	*Royal George*
Ruthenia	*Athenia*	*Arcadian*
Bermudian	*Caribbean*	*Zeeland*
Alaunia	*Franconia*	*Corinthian*
Ivernia	*Canada*	*Virginian*
Scandinavian	*Monmouth*	*Andania*
Sicilian	*Manitou*	*Saxonia*
Montezuma	*Tyrolia*	*Grampian*
Lapland	*Tunisian*	*Lakonia*
Cassandra	*Laurentic*	*Montreal*
Florizel (joined off Cape Race)		*Scotian*

At 2.30pm on Saturday 3 October HMS *Charybdis* made the following signal to the troopships: 'Have cables hove short. All ships in column Z will raise anchor at 3pm, and proceed, keeping column formation, steaming at 9 knots following leading cruiser *Eclipse*.' Promptly at 3pm, the *Eclipse* led column Z out of the anchorage, followed by *Diana* with column Y, including the *Royal Edward*, and in due course astern of them came *Charybdis* leading column X. HMS *Talbot* brought up the rear of the long column, which had a total length of 21½ miles;

HMT *Royal Edward* of 'Y' (White Squadron). *Author's collection, source unknown*

GREAT EUROPEAN WAR, 1914—1st Canadian Expeditionary Force

Numbering 33,000 Officers and Men.
Assembled at Valcartier, Quebec, August, 1914
Embarked for England at Quebec, Sept. 26th, 1914.
Landed at Plymouth, October 16th, 1914.

SHIPS OF CONVOY.
H.M.S. "MAGNIFICENT."

H.M.S "ECLIPSE," G.R.H.U.   H.M.S. "DIANA," G.R.D.H.   H.M.S. "CHARYBDIS," G.Q.R.M (flagship)

1. Megantic	HPCF	12. Carribean	LVCN	22. Tunisian	RNLC		
2. Ruthenia	RPQM	13. Athenia	VQRT	23. Arcadian	RJQT		
3. Bermudian	HEPK	14. Royal Edward	HMDR	24. Zeeland	HJLD		
4. Alaunia	JDKM	15. Franconia	HSDC	25. Corinthian	KQHH		
5. Ivernia	RNJB	16. Canada	PLMN	26. Virginian	HCJC		
6. Scandinavian	QDST	17. Monmouth	RTBP	27. Andania	JCPL		
7. Sicilian	RKBU	18. Manitou	PWJE	28. Saxonia	RPNQ		
8. Montreal	RSKQ	19. Tyrolia	RLVM	29. Grampian	HLKW		
9. Lapland	LJSN	20. Scotian	HSKG	30. Lakonia	RGMC		
10. Cassandra	HJBC	21. Laurentic	HNML	31. Montezuma	RHKW		
11. Florizel	HNLT			32. Royal George	HLTW		

H.M.S. "AARON."   H.M.S. "GLORY," G.R.P.T.

Rear Cruiser: H.M.S. TALBOT, G.V.C.L.

the last ship did not pass the entrance until 6pm.

The weather was perfect. It had been a fine autumn day, and as the land disappeared astern in a setting sun, ahead rose a full moon. It must have been a wonderful sight, and it certainly moved one young soldier in 16 Battalion (the Canadian Scottish that was to be), as he saw Canada disappear from sight astern, to write that, 'I'm proud of being a Canadian.' His words on going off to fight for King and Country might well be taken to heart by his fellow countrymen today. Pride in one's country seems to be the exception rather than the rule these days.

Once formed, the convoy proceeded at 10 knots. On Monday morning, 5 October, off St Pierre Island, HMS *Glory* joined. Then, as the convoy passed Cape Race on the same day, the *Florizel*, with the Newfoundland Contingent, joined the convoy. While it proceeded on its way, other ships were also moving into position. The *Princess Royal* (battlecruiser) left Scapa Flow early on the 3rd and reached the rendezvous on the night of the 7th; the battleship *Majestic* had arrived a day earlier. Off the American coast the *Suffolk*, *Niobe* and *Caronia* kept watch on the German liners lying in port. The Admiralty's plan was in action, and the grey ships of war were in position, ready to deal with the enemy.

It seems almost incredible that such a thing could happen, but apparently no one thought to tell the Admiralty that the convoy had sailed. By 6 October it was not sure whether the Minister's views on the escort had held it up or not. The previous day the C-in-C Home Fleet asked if the convoy had sailed, so the Admiralty made a signal to Rear-Admiral Wemyss to 'report what is position of convoy. Have you assembled and sailed?'

His reply was made at 6am and was received during the afternoon of the 6th. It read, 'Convoy assembled and left Gaspé Bay on October 3rd. Present position 45.40 N, 52 W, speed 9 knots.'

The Minister had informed the War Office that the convoy had sailed, but his message of 4 October did not reach the Admiralty until the 6th. As a result this great convoy was at sea for three days without anyone at Whitehall knowing about it.

The *Princess Royal* and *Majestic* spent 2½ days waiting at the rendezvous, all due to the assumption that the convoy would sail on 1 October, at 10 knots, as signalled by Rear-Admiral Wemyss before sailing. In fact it sailed on the 3rd and proceeded at 9½ knots, but nothing appears to have been done to correct the information. He was in touch with both ships by wireless on the 7th, and sighted them at dawn on the 10th.

On the 12th the *Princess Royal* dropped back, then cleared for action, and, with her band playing 'O Canada' and 'The Maple Leaf Forever', steamed up between columns Y and Z at 22 knots. It must have been a most stirring sight.

It had originally been planned to carry out the disembarkation of the troop transports at Southampton, which was being used almost entirely as a military port. By the end of September U-boats were being reported in the Channel, so it was considered safer to land the First Contingent at some port in the West of England. Devonport was decided upon, but after a visit by members of the Southampton Embarkation Staff, who made an adverse report, Southampton was finally selected and Rear-Admiral Wemyss was so informed on 6 October.

Certain camp equipment, without which the troops could not be dealt with ashore, was stowed in the *Montreal*, travelling at 12 knots, and the *Alaunia*, 14 knots – it was essential that these two should be unloaded first. These two ships, escorted by the *Diana*, parted company with the rest of the convoy 570 miles west of Scilly at 6.30pm on 11 October. As the rest of the convoy approached the longitude of the Fastnet, the escorting cruisers heard what appeared to be strong German wireless calls, and Rear-Admiral Wemyss decided not to break up the convoy.

As the convoy reached the longitude of the Fastnet, there occurred an event that upset all the plans. On 12 October the French had sighted a submarine off Cap Gris Nez and had established a patrol from Cherbourg to the Owers Light Vessel east of Portsmouth; in spite of this a submarine was sighted and attacked by one of the torpedo boats of the Portsmouth Extended Defence at 4.30pm on 13 October, at the east end of the Isle of Wight.

The presence of this submarine so near Southampton made that port dangerous for the disembarkation, and the Admiralty ordered the convoy to take shelter in Plymouth Sound until the road to the Needles could be cleared. The same orders were sent to the *Diana*. Her two transports arrived at Devonport at dawn on 14 October. At the same time Rear-Admiral Wemyss, who had reached Scilly, broke up the convoy and sent the first group to Plymouth, following with the other groups. All arrived safely during 14 October. Meanwhile, at the suggestion of the Commander-in-Chief, Portsmouth, orders had been given to the transports not to wait, but for them to carry on disembarking at Plymouth until the submarine in the Channel could be disposed of, and disembarkation officers were sent from Southampton to assist. The submarine situation did not improve and the disembarkation at Plymouth, having once started, continued until the whole convoy had landed at Devonport.

The submarines sighted on 12 and 13 October in the approaches to Southampton had, in fact, been dispatched from Germany with the special mission of attacking the convoy. On 8 October the German Admiralty had learned from their New York agents that 24 transports, escorted by eight warships, had left Quebec on the 2nd, a report that, so far, was very nearly accurate. Boulogne was assumed to be the destination of the force, the date of arrival to be 10-12 October, and, as the troops were thought to be sufficiently trained to take the field at once, the military authorities wished to have this convoy attacked. Accordingly, *U8* and *U20* were dispatched on 10 October to operate off Boulogne against it. It was *U8* that was seen off Cape Gris Nez, and *U20* was met off Culver Cliff, but neither submarine seems to have come as far west as Plymouth, and thus the convoy escaped a very real danger.

One of the troopers aboard the *Franconia*, a member of the same flotilla as the *Royal Edward*, was Private William Peden, who has vivid memories of Canada going to war. This is his account:

'At the outbreak of World War 1, I was working for the Grand Trunk Pacific at Portage-la-Prairie. Four days later, which I think was August 14th 1914, I enlisted with the local militia unit there, namely the 99th Manitoba Rangers. Other units throughout the district were raised under their various militia names from Brandon, Winnipeg, Fort Francis, Port Arthur and Fort William, which on reaching their quota were entrained together, and on reaching Val Cartier, Quebec, were amalgamated to form the 8th Battalion, 90th Winnipeg Rifles.

The make-up of the unit was composed mostly of men of Old Country extraction, many of whom, like the PPCLIs, had seen service with the British Army in India and South Africa, and some with the Royal Navy. The others, like myself, had no previous military experience, but they had one thing in common, all were young and, apart from the patriotic motive and the spirit of adventure, there was the opportunity of visiting their homeland and of seeing again the parents and relatives they had left behind, when emigrating to Canada. Whatever the reason they had for enlisting, they were second to none in the front line, and a great many were destined to never return.

Our brief training in Canada was done at Val Cartier Camp, where we were issued a

Private William Peden 1023, 8th Battalion, 'Little Black Devils', Canadian Expeditionary Force.
Hugh Peden

leather harness named the Oliver equipment, the Ross rifle, of cursed memory, a new fitting uniform with the appropriate badges and insignia of our Regiment, putties for the legs, instead of the black leather leggings we had on arrival – so that we began to look like a combat unit, at least we were all dressed alike.

PS I should make mention here of the cute little winter coats provided by Sir Sam, which were quietly and quickly removed on our arrival in France. The coats, if I remember rightly, had no sleeves, just arm-holes, so that they could be pulled over the tunic. They were made of bits and pieces of all the hair-growing animals and had just as many colours; the hair was still on and to the outside. God knows whose addled brain conceived them; when worn we looked like an army of cavemen, out after a few heads.

Our training of course was very basic, as we had to start from scratch, the usual parade square drill, route marches and learning to handle our weapons, and shooting on the ranges.

In the meantime a great armada of ships was assembling at Quebec City, perhaps the greatest in history, consisting of 30 transports and ten battleships; then came the day: "Orders to embark" and we left Val Cartier for Quebec, and to the waiting ships. As the ships were loaded they moved out to Gaspé Bay and took up their assigned positions in three lines 400 yards apart each way, and with the arrival of the last transport, the whole fleet, guarded on all sides with cruisers, moved off for Britain.

(I think Hugh came out to Canada on the *Laurentic*, while we came out on the *Grampian* – tonnage around 5,000 and old boats even then. I remember taking Hugh's passage papers to him. He was working for a farmer and at the time he was driving an old white horse rolling a field when I arrived. He cut quite a few capers and the old horse must have thought he had gone crazy.)

The crossing took 21 days as the regular shipping lanes were avoided due to the fear of submarines, and also to the fact that we could only travel as fast as the slowest boat and some of those were pretty ancient. During the day the naval convoy was scarcely visible, ranging widely on all sides of the carrier vessels, closing in towards nightfall. The trip itself was uneventful, with the exception that one day a sailor on the *Royal Edward*, which was the boat immediately ahead of us, fell overboard. As he was a good swimmer and clearly visible in the water, and to avoid running over him, the ships following veered out of line and came to a stop. Fletcher and I were on the top deck at the time and between us heaved a life-belt to him, which when it hit the water ignited a flare so that at night it could be easily spotted. However, he had quite a choice as there must have been half a dozen tossed over to him; selecting the most convenient he dived under and came up with

the belt encircling him, and resting his arms across it waited for our lifeboat, which had been immediately lowered, to pick him up, finishing the rest of the voyage aboard our boat the *Franconia*.

This incident; whatever signal had been flashed, brought the destroyers tearing in through the lines and for a brief few minutes we had a chance to see the Navy in action. As we neared Britain we were met by the heavier battlecruisers, which was quite a sight, and escorted into Plymouth. As you will note the crossing took 21 days and some time towards the end of October we arrived in Plymouth.

From Plymouth we entrained for Salisbury Plain. What a surprise – due to the heavy rains the camp was just a sea of mud and it still continued to rain. It was impossible even to keep the inside of the tent dry. We tried ditching around and even through the inside of the tent to try and drain the water off, but, if successful, only passed it along to the neighbour next door who was not slow in letting you know what he thought of you, as he had more than he could handle of his own.

The whole camp was just a slithering mess of mud and our nice soft Canadian brown shoes quickly took on the appearance of soggy moccasins with turned-up toes. In fact it was so bad that when I got my leave at New Year to go to Scotland, I walked out of camp with an old pair of shoes, exchanging them for a dry pair which I had in my kitbag after I got out of the mud. Here be it noted that while we were wallowing around in the mud, the British troops were in nice comfortable barracks – this of course was not due to prejudice or intent, but rather the lack of foresight on the part of Sir Sam.

How we fared for food I have little recollection, but I do remember one incident when the orderly officer came around one morning asking "Any complaints?". I told him the porridge was burned. Sticking his finger into my mess tin and licking it off, smacking his lips, he replied, "I like that burned taste." After that I had no complaints.

We were, however, supplied with a generous amount of what was termed "Iron Rations" – bully beef and hard tack – which was well named and I suspect it also was left over from the South African War or the Rile Rebellion; the bully beef, as it was named, was good Fray Bentos, and came in handy when on the move, but when one got it everyday in the soup it began to loose its appeal. As to the hard tack, I have seen men with poor teeth putting it in their haversack and pounding hell out of it with the butt of their rifle then scooping the chips into their mouth. So much for the food. We survived. Added to the misery of the camp condition, in which we were practically imprisoned, was the fact that on our arrival, the great military genius Sir Sam Hughes had placed all adjacent villages to the camp "Out of Bounds" to the troops. As we had no wet canteens, all the soldier could do when off duty was to try and keep warm, the comfort of a glass of beer and a chat with his buddies being denied him also. Sir Sam was opposed to wet canteens.

This stupid Bastard into whose care the Canadian people had entrusted the lives of some 30,000 men, must have had the idea that these were his personal contributions to the Great War, and as such were under his command to equip and manipulate as he saw fit, and in pursuing this idea, was continually at odds with the British.

I recall a muster parade, called by General Alderson, who was in command at that time, addressing the troops in which he stated that he was leaving for London to request that unless canteens be granted, he would resign his command, as he had no wish to command an army of men which were being treated as schoolboys. This address and statement to the troops is on official record. The outcome of his visit to headquarters was that canteens were established. This must have upset the micro mind of Sir Sam, but it was an order and he had to carry it out, and this is how he did it. One small tent, the ordinary bell tent, was set up. This was the canteen – it was open only at noon for an hour. The men lined up with their mess cans into which a pint was sloshed and had to be paid for, with the result that when time was up those at the end of the line did not get served and lost their dinner also.

This did not concern me too much, but at the request of the older buddies, who needed a drink, I would line up and, if lucky, turn it over to them. Sir Sam seemed to have the idea that this was his private army and hated the thought of having to conform to British standards, so that it could function smoothly as a unit within the Imperial forces.

The Oliver equipment, the rations, the shoes, the rifles, which were thrown away with curses at Ypres – my own rifle, after I was wounded, I turned over to another man, who was kicking the bolt of his rifle with the heel of his boot, to try and extract a spent shell – all were discarded and replaced by British equipment.

In the meantime, huts were hurriedly being erected into which we were moved around the turn of the year. Our next move from there was to France and the beginning of a new experience.'

The following passage is from Admiral Jellicoe's *The Grand Fleet 1914-16* (Cassell & Co, 1919), pp 137-139:

'On October 3rd 1914 all the ships of the Grand Fleet took up pre-arranged positions designed to secure a close watch over the northern portion of the North Sea, partly with a view to an interception of all traffic, and partly to ensure that no enemy vessel broke out of the North Sea during the ensuing week. The main object was the protection of an important convoy of Canadian troops, which was crossing from Halifax, and which the battlecruiser *Princess Royal* and the battleship *Majestic* had been sent to meet and to protect. The *Princess Royal* arrived at the rendezvous at 8pm on October 7th, and waited for the convoy, which was two and a half days late.

The Grand Fleet was disposed for this purpose during the period 3rd-11th approximately as follows:

The 1st Battle Cruiser Squadron was watching the Fair Island Channel from the western side.

The 2nd Battle Cruiser Squadron, with armed merchant-cruisers, the *Sappho* and three mine-layers, was stationed to the northward and eastward of the Shetland Islands.

The 1st Light Cruiser Squadron patrolled the northern portion of Area No 4.

The 2nd and 3rd Cruiser Squadrons patrolled Area No 5.

The 10th Cruiser Squadron also patrolled Area No 5.

The mine-sweepers patrolled to the eastward of the Fair Island Channel.

The Dreadnought Battle Fleet, with its divisions widely spread, worked to the northward of Area No 5, and the 3rd Battle Squadron to the northward of Area No 4, whilst the 6th Battle Squadron was utilised to watch the waters between the Dreadnought Battle Fleet and Norwegian territorial waters.'

The destroyers were stationed, some to guard the eastern approaches of the Pentland Firth, some to work off the Norwegian coast, and the remaining available vessels to work with the Battle Fleet for screening and boarding purposes. They returned to the bases (Lerwick or Scapa) as necessary for refuelling, and for shelter when the weather necessitated it.

The *Princess Royal* met the Canadian convoy on 10 October. On the 11th the Dreadnought Battle Fleet passed to the westward of the Orkneys, remaining there until daylight on the 12th, then returned to Scapa, the 2nd Battle Cruiser Squadron, with the *Teutonic*, being withdrawn from the patrol north of the Shetlands to a patrol line north-west from Sule Skerry lighthouse during the night of the 11th, remaining there until daylight on the 13th, when it left for Scapa. During 12 October all other vessels engaged in this operation returned to their bases for fuel, except the 3rd Battle Squadron (the ships of which had coaled two at a time during the operation) and the cruiser squadrons, which had been relieved as necessary to fuel.

Once in the hands of Government and Empire, the *Royal Edward* was used for interned enemy aliens for several months. When Mr John B. Jackson, of the American Embassy in Berlin, visited Britain to report on the treatment of German prisoners of war in England, he inspected the *Royal Edward* during its time as an internment vessel. In his report he stated:

'Of the ships, the *Royal Edward* was obviously the show ship. On board, the interned were separated into three classes dependent to a certain extent upon their social standing, but to a greater extent to their ability to meet extra expenses. Prisoners were permitted to avail themselves of the regular first-class cabins upon payment in advance of from 5s to 2s 6d a week, according to the number of persons occupying a cabin. At that time the ship was lying off Southend, and Mr Jackson reported that all the prisoners were locked below decks at night, which caused some nervousness among them owing to the apprehension of danger from Zeppelins.'

The envelope of a POW letter posted from the *Royal Edward*.
Author's collection, source unknown

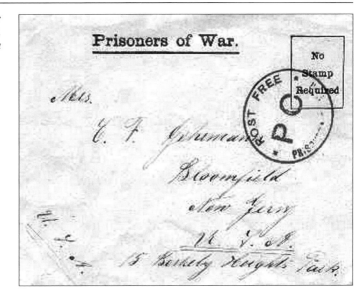

Then for a year both the 'Royals' carried soldiers, livestock and supplies heading for the battlefields of Europe – young men, all dressed in their shiny new uniforms and shiny new boots, with sweethearts and mothers to wave them off at the quayside.

The crews of the Mercantile Marine were the men who kept these magnificent steamers running, although the prospect of heading through hostile waters in a defenceless cruise-liner must have seemed very daunting, even to the bravest of souls.

4
To Gallipoli

Winston Churchill is widely credited as the man who committed British, French and – above all – untested Australian and New Zealand forces to the ill-fated campaign to seize control of the Dardanelles Straits and western Turkey in 1915. Indeed, although it was Churchill's drive and aggressiveness – not to mention cunning – that resulted in the campaign actually taking place, the notion of capturing the Turkish Dardanelles Straits had long been given consideration. It was widely believed, however – at least in professional circles – that a purely naval attempt to win the Straits was bound to end in failure.

But why attempt the Straits in the first place? The answer lay in the great strategic value that control would give the Entente Powers. The Straits linked the Mediterranean Sea with the Sea of Marmora. This not only gave ready access to the Turkish capital Constantinople and much of the Turkish Empire's industrial powerhouse, but also provided a lane to the Black Sea.

Just as importantly, if not more so, access to the Sea of Marmora was bound to give Britain and France supply route access to their eastern ally, Russia. Therefore it was quite feasible that should Britain and France gain the Straits they could succeed in not only eliminating Turkey from the war, but also in drawing Greece and Bulgaria into the war against the Central Powers.

Control of the Dardanelles Straits was therefore a prized ambition of the Entente Powers. As might be expected, given the huge tactical and strategic value placed upon the Straits, they were heavily defended, chiefly by natural geography. To the north they were protected by the Gallipoli Peninsula, to the south by the shore of Ottoman Asia. In addition, fortresses were well positioned on cliff-tops overlooking shipping lanes.

It seemed obvious to the Entente Powers – chiefly Britain – that no attempt upon the Straits could be considered without support from ground troops. The Greek Government, led by Eleutherios Venizelos, was of the same opinion. As soon as the First World War was under way, Greece approached Britain and offered to provide some 60,000 troops to assist in a combined land operation, the whole to be aided by old battleships as necessary.

However, both the British and French Governments – in this case in the form of British Foreign Secretary Sir Edward Grey – were initially opposed to any form of action. Grey retained hopes of bringing Turkey – at that stage still a neutral power – into the war on the side of the Entente Powers, in spite of mounting evidence of increasing (and well established) German influence in Constantinople.

In the event Turkey finally entered the war by siding with Germany and Austria-Hungary in late October 1914. By this time Venizelos's Government in Greece had fallen and the latter's previous offer of assistance was qualified by a requirement for additional Bulgarian support – which was not forthcoming.

In the meantime both Britain and France were finding news from the campaign on the Western Front sober reading. While much of their time, effort and resources were consumed by the requirements of the struggle in France and Flanders, both Governments gradually came round to the notion of opening up another front in the Mediterranean, one that offered possibly better prospects of success. In Britain in particular a number of members of the War Cabinet had long favoured decisive action away from the stagnation of the Western Front's lines of trench warfare.

Such 'Easterners' – which included future Prime Minister David Lloyd George – embraced a plan put forward by Churchill in January 1915 to attempt a naval capture of the Straits. Churchill took great care in placing such a proposal before the Cabinet. He coerced Admiral Sir Sackville Carden – the commander of British naval forces in the Mediterranean – into sending him a detailed plan for a solely naval attack upon the Straits. Carden obliged but was by no means personally in favour of such an approach. Nevertheless Churchill placed Carden's plans – which were sufficiently detailed to gain credence – before his War Cabinet colleagues on 13 January 1915. At this time the War Cabinet was somewhat despondent by the patent lack of success in France and Flanders, and further dismayed by a call by the Russian Commander-in-Chief, Grand Duke Nikolai, for radical action to offset pressure in the Caucasus. Thus Churchill received from Herbert Asquith's War Cabinet general agreement that action in the Dardanelles be given active consideration.

Notwithstanding an obvious desire to initiate any plan likely to bring with it a possibility of success, Admiral John Fisher's silence at the War Cabinet meeting was remarkable. As First Sea Lord his naval force was to take prime responsibility in driving forward Churchill's strategy. Given his later violent objections – which ultimately led to his (and Churchill's) resignation – his lack of objection in January was all the more surprising. It is possible, however, that he envisaged any eventual attack taking the form of a combined naval/ground troop undertaking.

Churchill came away from the Cabinet meeting believing that he had been given the authority to place Carden's blueprint into effect. In doing so he planned to make use of 'spare' aged battleships (thus raising Fisher's hackles). He set a date of 19 February for implementation of a first attack, plans that were formally approved by the War Cabinet on 28 January. Churchill's ambitious approach was, however, questioned by those who believed that it remained unclear in terms of strategy in the event of an immediate decisive breakthrough.

So much for British political opinion. In Paris the Government remained enmeshed in affairs on the Western Front and was somewhat less inclined to wholeheartedly support any British-sponsored expedition to the Dardanelles. Nevertheless the incoming French naval minister, Jean Augagneur, took a political gamble when he effectively disregarded the opinion of his professional advisers in backing the British plan. To some extent this was driven by a decided unwillingness to cede the possibility of a notable breakthrough to the British alone: the French Navy needs must share in any potential naval glory. A French squadron was consequently added to the February operation.

By this time Admiral Fisher was growing thoroughly alarmed at the prospect that 'spare' shipping be drawn away from his beloved Grand Fleet – a threat in being in the North Sea – for what he regarded as a highly dubious undertaking in the Mediterranean. His former close relations with Churchill – who had brought him out of distinguished retirement in October 1914 to his former post of First Sea Lord – began to chill. However, Fisher's growing reservations were largely ignored by British war minister Lord Kitchener. On 16 February 1915 Kitchener issued orders to ensure the readiness of Britain's sole available infantry division to assist with operations as necessary. He further specified that Australian and New Zealand forces stationed in Egypt en route for France should be made available if required. On 18 February the French Government similarly added a corps of men to the endeavour, although they arrived too late to be used the following day.

The first attempt upon the 65km-long, 7km-wide Straits was made on 19 February 1915 by a considerable number of combined British and French battleships comprising the new battleship *Queen Elizabeth*, three battlecruisers, 16 pre-Dreadnoughts (including four French vessels), four cruisers, 18 destroyers, six submarines, 21 trawlers, and the seaplane carrier *Ark Royal*. Overseeing the effort was Carden. Pounding the outer fortresses, the British and French attack proved ineffective in the face of an efficient Turkish defensive system and poor Allied gunnery, although greater damage was inflicted than the bombarding naval forces realised.

A renewed bombardment the following week, on 25th February (following a pause for adverse weather), was similarly unsuccessful. While the outer forts were themselves seized, the Allied force could not effectively silence the Turkish mobile batteries that poured shellfire from the heights.

Having paused to consolidate following the clear failure of February's attempts to batter the Turkish protective fortresses, a further naval effort was briefly launched on 18 March in an attempt to force through The Narrows (so-named because just 1,600 heavily-mined metres separated the shores on either side). However, immediately before the attack's launch Carden collapsed from nervous exhaustion. He was replaced by Sir John de Robeck. The renewed attack proved a heavy failure, chiefly on account of the presence of an unsuspected Turkish minefield. It was increasingly clear that ground support was required. A month's pause in operations was undertaken pending preparations for Allied landings at Helles and what was to become known as Anzac Cove.

Some 18,000 French colonial troops were dispatched to the region on 10 March – prior to the attempt on The Narrows – and on the 12th Lord Kitchener appointed Ian Hamilton (a former protégé) as regional Commander-in-Chief, responsible henceforth for the success of the expedition, accompanied by a force of 75,000 comprised largely of untested Australian and New Zealand troops. Hamilton, unsure of the appropriate strategy, sought advice from de Robeck and agreed on 27 March to a straightforward invasion of the Gallipoli Peninsula.

Preparations for the Allied landings were not auspicious, and were distinguished by hesitation, indecision and confusion. Meanwhile Turkish defences were further boosted by the arrival of ground forces around the Straits. As a measure of the extent of German influence over Turkish policy, regional command was placed in the hands of Liman von Sanders, who brought with him approximately 84,000 troops, which he dispersed to strategic locations around Gallipoli. As it transpired, however, Liman's careful positioning of his men was found wanting once Hamilton actually launched his attack on the southern peninsula: Hamilton chose to attack where the Turkish concentration was as its weakest.

The landings were initiated on 25 April 1915 but were largely mismanaged. But for the relative weakness of Turkish strength on the southern peninsula, the whole operation might well have been thrown back into the sea. As it was, heavy casualties were incurred at those locations where Turkish defenders were available in any force. Even so, two beachheads were established by Hamilton's force, at Helles on Gallipoli's southernmost tip (led by Sir Aylmer Hunter-Weston), and further up the coast near Gaba Tepe – the latter soon to be renamed Anzac Cove in honour of the Australian and New Zealand corps who bore the brunt of operations in the area (led by the rather more competent Sir William Birdwood). Having established two beachheads at great cost, Hamilton determined to extend the Allied position in the south, with attacks directed towards Krithia. Unduly optimistic in their aims, three successive operations were launched upon Krithia by Hunter-Weston in April, May and June 1915, but all were thrown back by Liman's increasingly effective Turkish defence force.

Meanwhile, British First Sea Lord Admiral Fisher's dramatic resignation on 15 May 1915 over Churchill's handling of the Gallipoli campaign led to the latter's own downfall as he too resigned, his wartime political career apparently over. Churchill had earlier, on 23 March, reluctantly admitted to the War Cabinet the failure of the purely naval bombardment, denting his already frail political credibility.

It was clear that operations in Gallipoli were going badly. The newly formed Dardanelles Committee in London met on 7 June to consider what steps to take next. Agreement was reached to send additional forces to Hamilton, greatly reinforcing the Allied presence on the peninsula by some three divisions – a decision made by Kitchener in the face of fierce opposition from hard-pressed commanders on the Western Front. Unfortunately for the Allies, their Turkish opponents were bringing forward additional reserves at a greater pace than they themselves could manage, with forces dispatched from both the Palestine and Caucasian fronts.

Such an injection of additional Allied resources signalled another major offensive. When put into effect on 6 August 1915 it took the form of a three-pronged attack: a diversionary action at Helles; movement northwards from Anzac Cove towards Sari Bair; and the centrepiece of the offensive, a landing in force at Suvla Bay by freshly arrived divisions operating under General Sir Frederick Stopford. The idea was for Stopford's forces to link with the troops at Anzac Cove and make a clean sweep across the Gallipoli peninsula.

In the interim Hunter-Weston pressed on with further attacks directed towards Achi Baba in Helles. These were uniformly unsuccessful, maintaining Hunter-Weston's particular record of poor results since arriving on the peninsula. Meanwhile, to Hamilton's credit the landings at Suvla Bay achieved total surprise and Stopford made initial progress unopposed. However, the wider offensive rapidly lost momentum by 10 August as local command indecision – Stopford was particularly at fault – and lack of firm decision from Hamilton's headquarters took their melancholy toll, although fighting continued at Sari Bair until 12 August. The next morning, at sea off the islands of Nisyros and Kos, HMT *Royal Edward* would meet her fate.

Hamilton's position was an unenviable one. He had command of three beachheads – at Helles, Anzac Cove and Suvla Bay – but each was overlooked by high ground commanded by Turkish forces. Progress was therefore not only infeasible, but his forces found themselves under more or less constant heavy fire. By now rapidly losing credibility among local commanders and – worse – among his troops – Hamilton determined to try and make a break south from Suvla Bay to link up with Anzac Cove, a distance of some 5km. Consequently he provided additional resources to Suvla Bay, including a new set of commanders to replace the discredited structure already in place.

In spite of additional men and materials Hamilton's attacks against Hill 60 and Scimitar Hill in August 1915 came to nought. With Allied casualties running at around 40,000, an especially uncomfortable form of trench warfare settled in, a disastrous state of affairs for the Allied forces. Hamilton, feeling the pressure, requested a further 95,000 reinforcements from Kitchener in London. He was offered barely a quarter, 25,000. Confidence in the operation in London and Paris was dwindling. Nevertheless Churchill pressed both Governments to provide continued support. French General Maurice Sarrail suggested a combined offensive against the Asian coast, a proposal rapidly overturned by his Commander-in-Chief Joseph Joffre, who insisted upon retaining French focus on the Western Front.

Affairs outside Gallipoli began to intrude upon strategy in the region. The invasion of Serbia and plans for an extensive landing at Salonika exhausted resources from both the French and British Governments, with the latter offering to provide up to 125,000 troops (much against Kitchener's inclination).

Such were the demands for men intended for Salonika that forces were diverted away from Hamilton in Gallipoli, to the latter's great dismay. As it was, Hamilton was facing increasing criticism from London as grim news of the expedition reached home, together with complaints of his mismanagement of the campaign (from the Australian journalist Keith Murdoch among others).

Thus with the possibility of further reinforcements to the region seemingly ruled out, Hamilton received word on 11 October 1915 of a proposal to evacuate the peninsula. He responded in anger by estimating that casualties of such an evacuation would run at up to 50%, a startlingly high figure.

The tide was clearly moving against Hamilton. His belief in what was widely viewed as an unacceptable casualty rate in the event of evacuation resulted in his removal as Commander-in-Chief and recall to London at a meeting of the Dardanelles Committee on 14 October.

Hamilton was replaced by Sir Charles Monro, who lost no time in touring Helles, Suvla Bay and Anzac Cove upon his arrival on the peninsula on 28 October. His recommendation was prompt: evacuation, although this did not meet with Kitchener's approval, who travelled to the region to see the state of affairs for himself. Upon his arrival, however, Kitchener quickly reversed his thinking upon seeing the conditions facing the Allied force, and recommended evacuation on 15

November 1915, overriding arguments by senior naval figures Sir Roger Keyes and Rosslyn Wemyss to attempt a naval seizure once again.

The British Government, having prevaricated for several weeks, finally sanctioned an evacuation on 7 December. Unfortunately, by this stage a heavy blizzard had set in, making such an operation hazardous. Nevertheless the evacuation of 105,000 men and 300 guns from Anzac Cove and Suvla Bay was successfully conducted from 10-20 December 1915. The evacuation of 35,000 men from Helles was conducted from late December until 9 January 1916.

The evacuation operation was easily the most successful element of the entire campaign, with casualty figures significantly lower than Hamilton had predicted (official figures quote just three casualties). Painstaking efforts had been made to deceive the 100,000 watching Turkish troops into believing that the movement of Allied forces did not constitute a withdrawal.

Winston Churchill, however, viewed Monro's achievement with a somewhat jaundiced eye: 'He came, he saw, he capitulated,' he wrote of Monro, and the sneer has remained through the years to blight Monro's correct decision and remarkable follow-through.

Some 480,000 Allied troops had been dedicated to the failed campaign. British casualties (including imperial forces) amounted to approximately 205,000. French losses were estimated at around 47,000. Turkey incurred around 250,000 casualties.

The subsequent Dardanelles Commission established to investigate the expedition's failure produced its final report in 1919; its conclusions were regarded as insipid, with no figures (political or military), and heavily censured.

As Admiral Fisher wrote in a letter to Winston Churchill on 5 April 1915: 'Damn the Dardanelles! They will be our grave!'

* * *

Troops began boarding the *Royal Edward* on 28th July 1915 at Avonmouth, which was used by ocean-going liners that were too large to get any further up the River Avon to Bristol. She was bound for Mudros via Malta and Alexandria, with her cargo of government stores, soldiers from a number of regiments, and medical personnel for the Gallipoli campaign.

On the crew list for the *Royal Edward*'s final voyage was William Nimmo, who on his Particulars of Engagement stated that his previous ship had been the *Kioto*; however, I can find no record of such a vessel existing during that time – perhaps there had been a spelling error.

As sailors and soldiers were boarding the *Royal Edward* they may well have been given a small postcard that contained the following poem. The idea would have been to bolster their morale. However, given the somewhat fatalistic sentiments expressed in the last four lines, it is hard to see how that might have been achieved. It may even have been intended to be used as a rousing patriotic song.

Farewell, 'Royal Edward.'

O! how often through the purple mists
That clothe the coming night
I have seen the 'Royal Edward'
Pass, and vanish from my sight.
I have watched her glide where shadows lie,
A world upon the sea:
I have said, 'God speed the noble ship,
That takes my love from me.'
And now – her cargo, not of gold,
But of metal greater far, –
She has taken England's noblest sons,
And with them crossed the Bar,
O! Weep not for our heroes,
For God himself has said,
'Lay down thy life for others,'
So weep not for our dead.
Weep for the cowards, the careless,

Weep that spies should mar our land,
And rise, and rouse, and wake yourselves,
Hold out a loving hand
To every man in khaki,
But let the cowards feel
That honest scorn will reach as far

PARTICULARS OF ENGAGEMENT

Name of ship	*Royal Edward*
Name	William Nimmo
Age	24
Nationality (if British state birthplace)	Coatbridge
Home	56 Church St
Last ship served on board	*Kioto*
Discharge date	17 June
Year of discharge	1915
Date and place of this agreement	10am 18 June 1915, Coatbridge
In what capacity engaged	5th Engineer

Balance of wages

Amount of wages per calendar month	£13 10s
Amount of monthly allotment	£8 0s
Cause	Discharged [like all the men]
Paid on discharge	£7 18s 2d
Discharge date and place	27 July 1915, Avonmouth

Signature of crewman	*W. D. D. Nimmo*

Report of character

For ability	VG
For general conduct	VG

Note: Apart from William's signature, this form was completed by an officer and officially stamped accordingly. These particulars were supplied by Kathryn Atkin.

As the finest tempered steel.
So sleep, and wake in Paradise,
Dear hearts beneath the sea,
And just one tear for the noble form
That will ne'er come back to me.

PETRONELLA O'DONNELL
Published by G. K. Hancock,
Printer, Clevedon

While we have no record of Willie's time on board the *Royal Edward*, a soldier making the passage was Private Edward 'Teddie' Tuttle. Little did this

young man know at the time, but he was never to step on English soil again.

Some time during 1914 Teddie enlisted into the Norfolk Regiment, the 3rd (Special Reserve) Battalion (14). He enlisted at Great Yarmouth and gave that town as his address. On Saturday 8 August 1914 the 3rd Special Reserve was sent to Felixstowe. In addition to taking a hand in the defence of the Harwich coastline against a possible invasion, the Battalion had the duty of training and dispatching drafts overseas. It was practically debarred from going abroad as a battalion and the task demanded from it, as a Special Reserve, was a far more weary and thankless one. It had to accept thousands of recruits, equip and train them and, as

Private Edward 'Teddie' Tuttle. *Pauline Dodd*

soon as the men showed promise, draft them off to other regiments.

It seems that Teddie wanted to see active service, so he and some other Norfolk men volunteered to join the Essex Regiment and were in the draft of 24 July 1915. It was a custom in the Great War for a soldier to be issued with a different number when he changed regiments, so Teddie, who by this time had become Lance Corporal Tuttle, No 17596 of the Norfolk Regiment, became Lance Corporal Tuttle No 20637 of the Essex Regiment. (This arrangement was altered in 1920 when a soldier was given a regimental number on joining and kept it thereafter no matter to which other regiment or corps he was posted.)

A postcard with the postmark 'Devonport', dated 9.45am on 31 July 1915, and bearing a ha-penny stamp, addressed to Mrs E. Tuttle, Norwich Road, Mattishall, East Dereham, Norfolk, read:

'Dear Father & Mother,
Am sending a photo of ship have only an hour longer here as we sail tonight at 8 o/c Friday,
Much love, Ted
Don't expect letter just yet. Farewell.'

Despite Teddie's statement, the *Royal Edward*, under the watchful eye of Commander Peter Wotton RNR, set sail on the evening of Wednesday 28 July 1915 at around 20.00 hours, and was reported off the Lizard in Cornwall on the 29th. On the same day her sister ship, the *Royal George*, sailed with troops from Devonport for Gallipoli. Coincidentally, the day after the *Royal Edward* was spotted rounding the most western point of England, my father, Digby Hugh Oliff, was born in the village of Great Burstead in Essex.

* * *

Helen Fowlds was a Canadian nurse who travelled from Boulogne to Folkestone, then on to the Aegean aboard the hospital ship *Asturias*. Her

Diary makes interesting reading as it covers almost the entire time that the *Royal Edward* was at sea during her final voyage to Gallipoli. It is also interesting to note the number of Canadians in the Folkestone area, and how her description of the *Royal Edward*'s demise varies from official notes of the time.

Helen Lauder Fowlds was born on 28 October 1889 in Hastings, Ontario, just a month before William Nimmo. Helen and her brothers Don and Eric were the children of Frederick W. Fowlds and the former Elizabeth Sutherland. Their great-grandfather was Henry Fowlds, pioneer lumberman and founder of Crook's Rapids (later Hastings), Canada West. Helen received her education in Hastings and at Norwood High School. She graduated as a nurse from Grace Hospital, Toronto, just before the outbreak of the First World War.

Helen enlisted immediately, and by December 1914 was in Quebec City receiving military training. She and other nurses from Montreal and

Helen Fowldes. *Trent University Archive*

Toronto sailed for England aboard the SS *Zeeland* in February 1915, and on the 24th, in London, was attested to serve in the Canadian Overseas Expeditionary Force as part of the Canadian Army Medical Corps. Helen and some of her fellow nursing sisters spent close to a month in London awaiting their postings to hospitals in France and England. On 18 March she sailed to France to begin her active service. She spent one week at Le Tréport, then was posted at Wimereux, near Boulogne-sur-Mer, as a member of the No 1 Canadian Stationary Hospital.

In June 1915 it was decided that the nursing sisters would be moved to Abbeville some time in the summer. In mid-to-late July Helen was granted leave, and travelled to Scotland with Ida Smith, a Canadian nursing sister also serving at Wimereux. Upon their return, Helen learned that she was not to report back to Abbeville but was to sail for the East, her exact posting unknown.

She sailed from Folkestone on 1 August, and from mid-August until late 1916 was stationed on the island of Lemnos in Greece. During that time Helen kept an autograph book with notes from her friends.

She sailed from Lemnos on 31 January 1916 and, after almost a month in Cairo, arrived in Salonica, Greece, on 3 March. By the summer of 1916 Helen was suffering from a chronic respiratory infection. In late September 1916 she asked for a transfer and was able to leave the camp at Salonica on the 25th. She spent some time in Malta before arriving in England on 20 October.

Following an examination by the medical board, Helen was found to be debilitated 'due to the strain of her long service' and was granted rest leave at Cheyne Place. On 28 November 1916 a follow-up medical examination found her to be recovered and she was posted to a Canadian Red Cross Hospital at Bushey Park. It was here in February 1917 that Helen received notice that she was a recipient of the Royal Red Cross (2nd Class) in recognition of her valuable service in connection with the war. Her investiture took place at Buckingham Palace on 3 March 1917.

On 1 June 1917 Helen reported for duty at the Canadian Convalescent Hospital at Clarence House. She remained there throughout most of the summer and travelled with friends to the Lake District in late August 1917. From mid-September until early November she spent her leave in Canada, the first time she had been home since her departure in February 1915.

Upon her return to England, Helen was posted to serve at Buxton in Derbyshire. By March of 1918 she was suffering from bronchitis and was transferred to Northwood for five weeks convalescence. On 15 April 1918 she reported for duty at Matlock Bath, Derbyshire.

Following the signing of the Armistice, Helen returned to France in the winter of 1919, serving at Dax and Dunkirk, and travelling through Northern France en route to Germany. She also served in England for a time in the spring of 1919. On 23 May 1919 she sailed for Canada on the SS *Megantic* and continued to serve in hospitals in Toronto. The official end of her service came with the General Demobilisation on 31 October 1920.

On 25 April 1921 Helen married Captain Gerald Marryat who had served during the war with her brother Eric in the Canadian Engineers. They settled at Ashfield House in Hastings and Helen became a well-known historian and newspaper columnist. Helen Fowlds Marryat died on 16 June 1965.

Some of the words in Helen's Diary were difficult to decipher and have therefore, sadly, been lost in transcription.

'Hotel Metropole – Folkestone

This should be a good place to begin for I hope never to see it again. We arrived off the packet from Boulogne at 1200 noon – no one to meet us. Finally found the unit at the Metropole – Spent the afternoon shopping – but Folkestone is the last place on earth to shop in. We have as much as possible ready – but that's not saying much.

The Hotel is huge but the management is not up to much. The place is full of Canadians, at lunch I saw hundreds and so many of their wives, etc, are here too. We are billeted here so aren't paying the bills, thank goodness, for it would be rather expensive.

The whole town is filled with Canadians and such splendid big men as they are. I was far too busy watching their faces as they went by to pay attention to shopping. I met Reg Runnels, looking so big and brown and manly.

The town itself is quite large – and spreads away inland from the cliff and down along the seafront. We walked miles to the shops.

The coastline is not so pretty as that of France across the Channel.

Hospital ship *Asturias*

To begin with it is the largest hospital ship afloat, 12,000 tons. It has been running from Southampton to Le Havre all winter and this is only its second trip to the Dardanelles.

The cabins have been all knocked out and in their place are huge wards filled to overflowing with beds, swung on a central pivot, that move whenever you do. We are all on one side of the biggest ward with Queens on the other. The other unit is downstairs somewhere. It is anything but secluded but we are all together and have heaps of fun. It was very cold the first day out and we were all "damn near froze" as Clark says.

There are 24 English sisters belonging to the ship and quite a few RAMC men, besides all the ship's officers. On this last trip they went right up the strait until within 2 miles of Acha Buba and saw the battle shells fall all around them and they were in great danger. The wounded were brought down to them on rafts with only the first field dressing on. They

had 1,500 cases and 56 deaths on the way home.

They have huge wards and a very complete operating room with two tables, a dispensary, sterilising room and all the conveniences of a modern hospital.

4 August 1915

This is the anniversary ending the first year of the war. Who could have foretold a year ago that today would see us off the coast of Spain bound for the unknown East?

It has been an ideal day. There was early service 7.30 for Anglicans and they woke with great religious zeal about 7.00 and discussed everything under heaven till we were all awake and they had made many enemies.

The RCs had theirs at 10.00, and the heretics again at 11.30. The decks were jammed and only those in the bald-headed row of the penitent bench – according to taste – heard what the sermon was about. The Sisters were herded together on one small section of the deck. The padre exhorted us to celebrate the day fittingly so after it was all over we had beer for lunch.

About 12.30 we sighted land again and at 2.00 were off Cape St Vincent capped with its huge lighthouse and attendant buildings. The coast just there is high and rugged, but farther south slopes, to reveal a rolling country dotted with tiny villages. Everything is of white stone and shows up very plainly.

Just below the Cape is another prominent point with a signalling station, and beyond it a village – at the foot is a harbour full of fishing boats. Further inland are the Everlasting hills, half veiled in mist.

No wonder dreams are likened to castles in Spain, the very air makes one doubt the reality of things, the warmth of the sun dulls one's ambitions and it is a pleasure to sit and fancy what lies beyond that rather forbidding coast line. The air is heavy with the odour of bal of gile [?].

Have just been reading an Imperial Birthday Book compiled and edited by Miss [Clint], and in it came across Browning's "Home Thoughts" which had been in my mind all day:

"Nobly, nobly Cape St Vincent to the north-west died away.
Sunset, ran one glorious blood-red reeking Cadiz Bay
Bluish mid the burning water full in face Trafalgar Bay
In the dimmest south-east distance dawned Gibraltar, grand and grey.
Here and there did England help me, how can I help England? Say?
Who so turns as I this evening turns to God to praise and pray."

Farther on I came to a verse of Burns that I think would find its echo in most of our hearts:

"Home, home, home, home fair I be
O home, home, home – to my ain countrie."

"Gib." [Gibraltar]

We passed at 2.30am and to our surprise it was almost indistinguishable. In France it was broad daylight at 2.30. A faint outline of lights was visible – & on the Africa shore the illumination of a large city – Pautelleria – we passed the island in the middle of our famous game with the English sisters. A purplish misty cloud rested on it, obscuring the higher parts of it. It was formerly a convict settlement but now is covered with vineyards. It belongs to Italy. There was considerable vegetation and against it and in the slanting rays of the afternoon sun the white buildings showed with startling vividness. Off shore were some huge rocks & a smaller fortified island and lighthouse.

Malta

Pop 184,000, area 20 miles by 9¾ miles. The island [Ogygia] mentioned in the Odyssey where Ulysses is supposed to have been bewitched by Calypso. Also the [Milita] – where St Paul was shipwrecked & where he began a Christian church. A church now stands up in the place where he first set foot. The temple of the Knights of Malta is also here, and in it and other ancient churches is some of the most magnificent tapestry in the world. The great dome Musta is not in sight as we lie in harbour – or rather just outside the harbour in the bay. It is said to have been built without scaffolding. Valetta is in view all along this coast – a city of [?] with an English pop of about 10,000. In peace times it has a garrison of about 4,000 soldiers but at present no doubt it greatly exceeds this. It is the headquarters of Sir Ian Hamilton & the chief wireless station for the Mediterranean. Three huge stations are to be seen from here.

We reached here some time during the night and at 4.30 some of the girls were ambitious enough to get up. They said the white town in the early morning light looked like the ghost of a dead city.

The scene before us later when the sun rose was picturesque in the extreme. The clear blue water and tiny fishing boats with their snow white sails, the sand coloured island, the various types of architecture, the old native city beyond, and the new on the shore, only dating back to the 15th century & therefore of recent date, the fortifications, naval dockyards and other signs of a military and naval base, made a picture never to be forgotten.

We are drifting with the tide and the island is revealed in panorama before us. There is no point of great height on the island, and no vegetation except that resulting from artificial irrigation, which however is said to be very luxuriant.

A boat came out about 6am and asked if we wanted coal or water or provisions. We did not. Then they asked if we wanted to know the destination of the Canadian units and everyone on the boat shrieked wildly "Yes". Well it appeared they had no news for us and had to wireless to London to the War Office. By 10am they were back again with news that we were to proceed to Alexandria for orders. Great was the joy as we had feared one unit at least might be left behind at Malta.

While waiting for news a troopship bound for the harbour passed quite close to us. For a while the wildest cheering from boat to boat and cries of "Are we downhearted?" kept us in the public eye and then the little dispatch boat raced over to them and we were in a moment forgotten, every head turned to learn the news, and just as rapidly that in turn was forgotten and all the eyes were turned to the shore.

Farther off shore a 1st Class Battleship and a cruiser were to be seen, both French and on their way to the harbour as Malta is also a French naval base. The harbour of Valetta is of great natural strength beside the breakwaters and fortifications. Many of the forts etc date back to the days when the Knights of Malta held the Island against the Turks, and more recently when for two years the inhabitants aided by the British besieged the town and finally recaptured it from the French in 1804.

English is the language of commerce & English currency is in use though French and Italian gold is good. Italian is the language used in the courts and French is also spoken.

We had opportunity here to notice the intense blue of the water – less noticeable while in motion and as the boats drew near their keels and propellers were plainly visible through the clear water.

We rather hoped the natives would come out with lace, as the English sisters said they did the last trip of the boat. It may have been because it is Sunday but at any rate no one appeared.

The lace they bring out is of a rather inferior quality, and one has to haggle with them as at first their prices are exorbitant, but we all hoped to get a little if only as a souvenir.

The great dome Musta … [?] … supposed to have been built without any scaffolding, was not to be seen, but the [Templars] Church was and several native Mosques to give one an idea of the style.

We got under way again about 10am, everyone in great humour at the hope of going farther on toward the zone of activities. Mail was brought to us and ours taken away – however, no mail for us came with that.

Service began shortly after we were moving and it was very impressive. The men of our units were together on D deck, the RAMC on E. deck [aft] and the officers and sisters on E and the boat deck – never under any circumstances does the English service lose in power or seem anything but suitable and fitting. We were exhorted to remember, as we had sung, that indeed we were treading where the Saints had trod – and the lesson had to do with the journeyings of St Paul. The men all seem to have voices above the average and the hymns are always a delight.

It is now 12 noon and we are again out of sight of land, and another voyage of 2½ days lies before us, to Alexandria. No one regrets it for we are very happy indeed here and it will be a long long time before we are again among such pleasant people and living in such comfort.

Helen, en-route for Alexandria. *Trent University Archive*

Alexandria – Founded 331BC by Alexander the Great

Population 377,000 including 48,000 Europeans – 2nd city of Egypt. Fort [Rait] Bay – on the side of the famous 'Pharos' – a lighthouse built by Ptolemy II Philadelphus in 280-274 – originally 540 ft high. One of the seven wonders of the world. Statue of Mo Ali – in Place Mehemet Ali. Pompey's Pillar – 88 ft high including base – perhaps a Christian monument of victory – built about time of Theodosius I. Stands on site of famous temple Serapeum – dedicated to Serapis, the god of the lower regions. Catacombs of [Kow]-est-Shukaya (hill of potsherds) – an Egyptian burial place of 2nd Cent: A. W. [Leinn] in rocks. The tombs were discovered in 1900. They consist of several stories. Alexandria blend of Egyptian architecture [with] Graeco-Roman style. Probably tomb of some Egyptian Magnate [with] smaller chambers for family servants. A spiral staircase lighted by a large, round shaft descends near a sarcophagus-chamber of later date to two stories…

Later – After seeing Alexandria, we drove to the catacombs but as it was a native holiday no one was admitted. There was nothing to be seen from the outside except a modern cement floor in the midst of a waste of sand – with a very modern raised skylight, and some guards at the gate.

Pompey's Pillar marks the site of one of the most ancient temples but at present only the pillar and a small sphinx are to be seen. Nearby was a native cemetery. We could see the mourning women outside the gate sitting in the dust. Inside the people were swarming about the graves, which were marked by some sort of stone of pure glittering white. It was a very desolate looking place, just a waste of sand.

On that day we also drove along the Nile, or rather one branch of its many mouths – it was filled with boats loaded for Cairo. It was a mere stream as we saw it and very muddy. Along its banks grew date palms, and real palms, fig trees, the leaves exactly as art has shown them, and very dusty, bedraggled looking gardens.

The native quarters alone were worth the trip. It happened to be the native Christmas and the city was a blaze of colour. The flags are red with 3 white crescents. Over here the Red Cross is not much used as the natives object to it – a red crescent on a white ground being used instead.

The native dress is picturesque in the extreme, and Solomon in all his glory was not arrayed like one of these. They are ancient

The port of Alexandria in 1915, the final port of call for the *Royal Edward*. *Trent University Archive*

and modern combined, robes of bright orange, red, magenta, white, black and mixed, with stockings usually of a most incompatible shade, and often bright yellow European boots. The f[?] seems to be the universal head dress – it is lined with straw & seems to be very cool. Some of the dock labourers and boatmen wear turbans with openwork lace crowns, and others had crowns, made of large coconut.

Some of the men wore the baggy Turkish trousers and others just the long clinging robes. The women appear to have several layers of clothing but the outer is a long voluminous wrap of black. The upper class women wore veils over their faces, of white crepe de chine and the poor classes seemed to wear black. They don't all wear nose pieces.

The children are very bright looking, big brown eyes, and very white teeth, so dirty, and yet lovable.

The harbour is very large, divided into the East and West parts. There were about 30 ships, Turkish, German and Austrian interned. Of course commerce is practically at a standstill – in place of trading vessels and passenger steamers are battleships, transports, troopships, and as many as 8 hospital ships in harbour at once.

At the mouth of the harbour is a net for protection against submarines. No vessel is allowed to sail between sunset & sunrise. Several forts command the entrance.

The palace of the Khedive was quite near – an immense white building with modern striped awnings, brilliantly lighted at night. The harem is there too though this Khedive is said to have only one wife. His yacht lay in the harbour near us.

Egypt is British in name but the men on the ship all said that it was an open secret that if the Turks managed to hold the Dardanelles, and that England seemed to be getting the worst of it, Egypt would side with Turkey. Now, of course, they are all yelling for

England – our boatmen were most loyal, we noticed, in showing us the ships England had captured.

The shops are mostly on the Rue Che-P, Rue St Catherine, Rue de Rosette, one of the streets of ancient Egypt, and the Square de Mehemet Ali.

Raoul, of Paris & London, is the main shoe shop, Bryan Danies, a pocket edition of the Army & Navy, [Hammo], a French departmental store, Shuler's, the best place for books, a branch of Roger & Gallet's, where all sorts of toilet articles were obtainable, large native stores, curio shops, good jewellery stores, in fact Alexandria is a very up-to-date place to shop in.

The jewellery, with the exception of Egyptian curios, is much like what we saw in France. The Egyptian jewellery is very bizarre, mummy cases opening to reveal the mummy, baskets showing Moses inside [cup] of health and happiness & the key of the Nile, scarabs, real and imitation. I did not buy anything except a couple of [?] of Egyptian design, for so much is bogus, being manufactured in England or Germany. Many of the things were exactly the same as Aunt Hattie has sent us from China or Japan.

The hotels are fairly good. The Majestic, Savoy and Metropole are among the best. For the men there are excellent clubs.

The French gardens are wonderful, a mass of extravagant blooms of all colours, & all sorts of native animals and birds.

St Mark's is the principal English church, but there are several very interesting native mosques.

We spent practically four days at Alexandria as we anchored about 9am August 11th, and did not leave again till 1pm August 14th. However in that time we spent barely a day on land, as the first day no one was allowed ashore or the last day, and

another afternoon we spent waiting to be transferred from the *Asturias* to the *Delta*. The *Asturias* docked the afternoon of the 12th, and just across the pier from us was the *Franconia*, now used as a troopship. [The *Franconia* had arrived in England with the *Royal Edward* from Canada as part of the great Canadian 'flotilla'.]

While on the *Delta* we were near a transport evidently used as a base for submarines for two were moored to it, *B-11*, that did such splendid work at the Dardanelles, under St Holbrook, and *B-6*.

I must not stop without mentioning the heat. Personally I had come prepared to die of sunstroke within 24 hours. On the ship it was always fairly cool, but in the city the heat was intense. As we had considerable shopping to do we had to rush about a good deal, and suffered in consequence. I do not think it was as I expected, as I have felt pretty hot at home, but the air is so humid that one perspires excessively & in that way feels most uncomfortably sticky.

We saw the last of Alexandria about 2.30pm, its flat coastline broken by occasional palm trees and houses, fading away into the sea, and the last stage of our journey has begun.

The smells are as nothing compared to those in the streets of Staples, or parts of Boulogne.

Hospital ship *Delta*

Tonnage 9,000. Not nearly so large as the *Asturias*. Accommodation for 560 cases. On this last trip they carried 1,100, and left as many more laying on the shore.

They have been on this run since April 27th, which is since the beginning as the fighting began April 25th, and so they regard the *Asturias* as a mere newcomer and not worthy of consideration. Their destination is usually Alexandria but they have gone to England occasionally.

The meals are better and the service is better than on the *Asturias*. The Matron says that once the wounded are on board everyone, stewards, stewardess, ship's officers and everyone available cuts down dressings and helps in a general way. The crew is [mature] with a few exceptions and all the stewards and [waiters].

There are 14 sisters and 6 MOs and they all look awfully tired and over-worked. When they take wounded on, they work all the first day and night and all next day till midnight, when they go to bed till 6am. The Matron has asked for 4 from our units to go up to the peninsula and help them, but it is too much to expect to be one of the lucky ones. It would be the experience of a lifetime as the ship is constantly exposed to shellfire.

Lemnos

We first saw the Island at 8am on Monday, Aug 16. A high promontory to the left, a line of hills with valleys sloping to form a narrow shore at the right. Mudros Bay is a splendid natural harbour, practically unused till war broke out – now it is the headquarters for the fleets while in action and one of the busiest and most carefully guarded harbours in the Mediterranean. Like all the others it is guarded by a submarine net at the mouth.

We were all on deck with glasses as we steamed slowly in and the panorama unrolled before us. What at first had seemed part of the land soon appeared as the anchorage for fully a dozen battleships, completely concealed from view, except for the tops of the masts, and quite indisguisable at a distance. Besides there were hospital ships – hospital carriers, that is transports now being used as hospital ships – and all the etceteras war calls into being.

Our first impression of the land was a collection of tents enveloped in a sand storm. The tents may or may not have been a hospital, but that sand didn't look good to us. Further observation revealed several villages very [tiny], something with a black flag on it, and thousands of tents all over the island. Most of them were bell tents and are, it is said, used for troops.

The island is nothing but a sandy, rocky waste. There are a few trees to be seen but very few.

So far it has not been satisfactory having hospitals on land. There is no water except what comes from Alexandria or what is distilled on board ship.

The Headquarters ship the *Arragon* is lying quite near us, and is connected by private cable with the War Office, London. That is our only connection with the outside world and being purely official isn't of much use.

Yesterday afternoon a bulletin was posted stating that the *Royal Edward* had been torpedoed while landing troops and had gone down in four minutes. We saw her sail from Alexandria and waved to the men. One rumour says they were Canadians but that is not credible. Out of about 2,000 only about 500 were saved and taken aboard the Hospital Ship *Soudan*. We passed her on our way from Alexandria but she gave out no news.

Ordinary transports are being used constantly for carrying wounded & everyone here considers it a great risk. The *Allonia* left with 3,000 wounded and has not yet been reported safe, and the *Mauretania* is 6 days overdue from England.

We were transferred from the *Delta* to the *S[?]la*, a sort of hotel ship or distributing base for RAMC & Sisters. They are being sent on daily to hospital ships or carriers but so far only one Australian Hospital has settled on shore.

It is an old P&O boat and very dirty. Our unit is fairly well off in cabins – 4 in each and hot as blazes but we are sure of a certain amount of privacy. #3 [?] is partly settled and the rest sleep on deck. Some English sisters left today so there is more room now.

We found a lot of Toronto men among the RAMC men here and last night we had a wonderful time dancing and singing and talking over old times. They are all sore and very blue. They say the management down here is an absolute farce and that things are in a terrible state of chaos.

Last Sunday during the big fighting in the Peninsula between 40 & 50 doctors and 100 nurses were at [Imbros] on a transport. They could see the battle and knew that men were dying by the thousands and yet they were not allowed to go up. Within half a mile of them a transport with 2,000 wounded was lying –

Photographs of Helen and other young nurses. *Trent University Archive*

staffed by 4 Sisters and 2 MOs. They were all nearly crazy to help but knew nothing about the transport till after. Of course the authorities didn't think of sending them. The English sisters are just about crazy as many of them have been sitting around for about 3 weeks. Some of them were allowed to go and help on a carrier for 24 hours. At the end of that time in spite of the need for them they were recalled. One MO has gone to England on the [*Aquitania*] and he vowed he'd raise hell if he ever got there. The whole affair at the Dardanelles is said to be a frightful botch and not worth the men they are losing. Sunday's casualties alone were 14,000 at the lowest figure.

There is scarcely a breath of air here in Mudros Bay and we are all very hot. There is no ice and no drinking water except bottled Soda, but the meals are fairly good. The flies are terrible.

There is absolutely no chance of getting off the boat and no little boats to sail around in if one could get off.

The shore looks exactly like the northern coast of Africa, just a line of hills against the faint blue of the sky, and nothing but sand between them and the sea. A couple of the hills are quite high, 300-400 ft, but for the most part they are just high enough to shelter the harbour and keep off every breath of air. As I look at the shore now it is dancing in heat waves, and a very desolate, deserted looking place.

The *Africa* arrived this am and Col McKee had orders to disembark his men at once. He says wherever they go we will go too so that means the Island for us. Last night, Aug 18, there was a moon, and you'd never recognise the place. A little Scotch Sister said the scenery after 8pm was exactly like Scotland – the hills look so soft and purplish you could imagine them covered with heather and the bay is as smooth as any lake, but up to 5pm it is exactly like hell.

We are to have a 1,000-bed hospital on the west shore and in spite of everything the English sisters envy us. They are all destined for hospital ships and many of them are poor sailors.'

Records show that the *Royal George* called at Malta on 5 August and arrived at Alexandria on the 9th. The *Royal Edward* would have followed a day behind. The *Royal George* then sailed from Mudros harbour in Lemnos on 11 August, arriving safely on the 13th. The *Royal Edward* sailed from Alexandria on 12 August, also heading for Mudros. Apart from her crew of 220, she had on board 31 officers and 1,335 men. Even during a time of war, the two sister ships still shadowed each other.

5
Sinking

On the same day, 12 August 1915, the recently arrived German submarine *UB14* sailed from Bodrum for the known steamer route between Alexandria and the Dardanelles. She was under the command of Lt-Commander Heino von Heimburg with a crew of 14.

This small submarine of 127 tons, just over 90 feet long and less than 10 feet wide, had been completed at Bremen Dockyard earlier that year. She had been ordered by the German Navy on 15 October 1914, launched on 23 March, and commissioned on the 25th. I still find it strange to think of submarines in action during the First World War, yet it is clear that the Germans had a sophisticated building programme in place.

UB14's builders had been founded on 8 November 1843 as the Eisengiesserei und Maschinenfabrik Waltjen und Leonhard, becoming Waltjen & Co in 1849, and had only started in ship construction very slowly, with the *Roland* in 1846 and the *Falcke* in 1865. On 26 March 1873 the firm became part of AG Weser, and the very first important order came from the Kaiserliche Marine. Between 1875 and 1881 11 gunboats of the Wespe Class were built by the yard, after which construction was again mainly for civil use. Halfway through the 1880s serious dredging took place on the Weser River, again making Bremen an important harbour, and just before the turn of the century it grew quickly.

This was also the moment when AG Weser decided to buy new land at Gröpelingen, where it constructed five new slips. In 1904 everything was ready at the new location and Bremen was abandoned for further ship construction. New installations followed and between 1905 and 1914 no fewer then 40 passenger and merchant ships were constructed on the new wharf.

During the First World War the firm constructed small cruisers and U-boats. D'Equevilley, who had worked at the Germaniawerft yard, was asked by AG Weser to construct a new U-boat in 1912, and as it now had its own U-Bootkonstruktionsbüro it immediately became part of the Ms Type U-boat programme of the Marine-Amt. The first U-boats constructed were, however, not of the Ms Type but were UB I Class subs, the *UB 9-UB 15* series; UC I series and UB and UC II series were also constructed at Weser, and by 1917 most of the work went into the construction of the UB III Class. Three UC IIIs were ordered in 1917 also but were never finished; 14 more UB IIIs ordered in June 1918 were never started.

The company also built three U-boats for the Austro-Hungarian Navy, the *U15-U17* series, at Pola. AG Weser was also responsible for the plans of the *U 27-U 32* series and the *U 40* that were constructed at Pola and Fiume for the Austro-Hungarian Navy, and they also gave a licence for construction of three U-boats in Sweden: the *Bävern* was constructed at Kockums at Malmö, and the *Illern* and *Uttern* at the state naval shipyard of Karlskrona.

UB14 was transported in sections overland by train to Pola in Austria where she was reassembled in June 1915 to operate against British and Allied shipping in the Mediterranean. On 6 July she torpedoed and sank the Italian Armoured Cruiser *Amalfi* while operating under the Austrian flag off Venice. She then sailed for the Dardanelles on 16 July. This was at a time when the range of submarines

Above **A German UB submarine in dock. The UB14 was of a similar design.** *RD Designs*

Below **Another view of a First World War German submarine.** *RD Designs*

Photographs of the interior of *UB88*, a similar design to *UB14*.
RD Designs

The torpedo tubes are proudly displayed. Note the rear fin of a torpedo visible in the right-hand tube. *California Wreck Divers Association*

was very limited, unlike today. To reach Bodrum she had to be towed a considerable part of the distance by an Austrian destroyer. Even so, her engine broke down off Crete and her compass became defective. Despite these problems she arrived safely at Bodrum on 24 July. On arrival she recharged the batteries of the *UC14*, which had arrived four days earlier with engine problems. A maintenance team then had to travel from Constantinople to carry out necessary repairs to both submarines, a journey that was not easy to make at that time, being partly by train and partly by camel.

After leaving Bodrum on 12 August *UB14*'s first sighting that evening was of a fully lit hospital ship, which she did not attack. Then on the next day, Friday 13th, she first sighted the P&O liner *Soudan* in service as a hospital ship (later to act as a rescue vessel). It was then that she sighted the *Royal Edward* sailing unescorted for Mudros. This was too good to miss – a ship loaded with troops and arms heading for the battlefields, which would be seen as 'fair game' by any U-Boat commander. *UB14*'s captain took aim and fired one torpedo from less than a mile away, hitting the *Royal Edward* stern portside. Following a huge explosion the *Royal Edward* began to sink, and sink very quickly. The time was approximately 0920 hours. Official reports stated that her final position was given as being 6 miles west of the islet of Kandeliusa, or Kandhelioussa, 36°31′ N, 26°51′ E. The after deck

The only known image of *UB14* preparing for an attack. *Fortunes of War.com*

was awash in 3 minutes and the *Royal Edward* had sunk with her bows in the air in only 6 minutes.

Initial reports stated that 132 men were lost, including her captain, and that figure has been repeated in many publications up to the 1980s. In fact, the loss of life was far greater – perhaps such reports were referring only to those lost from the Mercantile Marine service. The *Dictionary of Disasters at Sea 1824-62* published by Lloyds Register of Shipping states that, 'Of the 1,586 on board, less than 500 were rescued.'

Just before the attack the troops had carried out boat drill, so when the torpedo struck many were below decks stowing their gear. Another account says that the men, who had undertaken a route march just before leaving Alexandria, were waiting on deck for foot inspection at about 9.20am when the torpedo hit. Their lifebelts were down below, and when the ship was unexpectedly struck most of them ran below decks to fetch the belts. Owing to the ship's sudden heeling over and sinking, these men never saw daylight again.

Those saved were picked up by the *Soudan*, two French destroyers and some Greek trawlers, most likely from Nisyros or Kos, which were near enough to the scene to help with the rescue operation. Another was the *Achilles*, which managed to rescue 29 survivors. Ironically, she herself was torpedoed and sunk on 31 March 1916 by *U-44*, 90 miles west-north-west of Ushant, with the loss of five lives.

The *UB14* did not harass the rescue ships. Her compass had become defective again, so she returned immediately to Bodrum in Turkey for repairs, arriving later that morning. Her day's work was done.

The hospital ship *Soudan* (*above right*), of the P&O Steam Navigation Company, was the first rescue vesel on the scene following the sinking of the *Royal Edward*. She was later joined by the *Achilles* (*right*), two French destroyers and various Greek fishing trawlers from nearby Nisyros and Kos.
A. Duncan/Author's collection, source unknown

The defenceless HMT *Royal Edward* holds the somewhat sad distinction of being the first conscripted ocean-going troop carrier to be destroyed by enemy fire in the 20th century. To partly replace the great loss of troops, another draft of 150 men of the Essex Regiment was dispatched the following month on 29 September.

* * *

The Times reported the loss on Tuesday 18 August:

'BRITISH TROOP SHIP SUNK

TORPEDO ATTACK IN AEGEAN

600 SURVIVORS

FEARED LOSS OF 1,000 LIVES

The Secretary of the Admiralty announced yesterday that the transport *Royal Edward* had been sunk by an enemy submarine in the Aegean Sea. The loss of life was apparently about 1,000, those on board numbering just over 1,600 and about 600 being saved. The following is the text of the Admiralty announcement: The British transport *Royal Edward* was sunk by an enemy submarine in the Aegean Sea last Saturday morning [it was actually Friday]. According to the information at present available the transport had on board 32 military officers and 1,350 troops, in addition to the ship's crew of 220 officers and men. The troops consisted mainly of reinforcements for the 29th Division and details of the Royal Army Medical Corps. Full information has not yet been received, but it is known that about 600 have been saved. Distressing scenes were witnessed at the Bristol offices, where, however, there was little information available.'

The Times report continued:

'FIRST ENEMY SUCCESS
OF THE KIND

Our Navy Correspondent writes: After a year's work which has been in all respects brilliantly successful, and for which no praise can be too high, the British Transport Service has had the misfortune to lose one of its finest vessels in a torpedo attack. There is something peculiarly distressing in the circumstances in which a thousand gallant souls are missing without an opportunity to strike a blow for their own safety or defence, and the ready sympathy of the nation will go out to the relatives and friends of those who have perished. At the same time, all who grasp the magnitude of our transport operations may well marvel that we have hitherto been spared such a disaster. That this first loss of a British transport should have occurred in connection with the operations at the Dardanelles is significant. The convoy of large bodies of troops through the Mediterranean, where not only German but Austrian submarines are known to be operating, must throw upon the Navy very heavy responsibilities. These are not lessened, moreover, by the fact that, as we have been told officially, only our surplus ships and vessels are being used in that theatre of war. This misfortune will serve to bring home to the country as nothing else could the marvellous work which has been done by the Navy and Mercantile Marine in conjunction in ensuring safe transport for the troops not only between these shores and the Continent, but to the Aegean, and from all our Dominions across the oceans. The last-named task was satisfactorily performed at a time when the German raiders were still at large, and it will be remembered that the

Sydney was actually convoying an Australian contingent across the Indian Ocean when she received by wireless news of the arrival at Cocos Island of the *Emden*. Mr Churchill said that approximately 1,000,000 men had been moved without any accident or loss of life. That was six months ago, and the number must have been doubled in the interval. The only occurrence modifying the late First Lord's remarks was the attempted torpedoing of the transport *Manitou* in the Aegean on April 17. The Turkish torpedo boat *Dhair*

Hissar escaped from Smyrna, stopped the vessel and ordered the troops to abandon her. Two torpedoes were fired, but missed and the torpedo boat was then driven off and run ashore by British destroyers, which had come up, the crew being captured. Owing to two boats being upset in leaving the transport 51 lives were lost.

For a parallel case to the loss of the *Royal*

News of the sinking affected all parts of the UK. Here is a newspaper cutting from the *Warrington Guardian* dated 21 August 1915. *Ros Pates*

LOST TRANSPORT

Local Men on the Royal Edward.

NEWS ANXIOUSLY AWAITED.

LETTERS FROM MALTA.

It is believed that several Warrington soldiers were on board the Royal Edward when she was torpedoed and sunk in the Ægean Sea on Saturday last. We have been able to obtain confirmation of the presence on the vessel of two local men, but, of course, no news as to their fate has yet been received. These are Privates Thomas Kaye, 17, Watkin-street, and William Hart, 3, Cyril-street. They are companions and members of the South Wales Borderers.

Letters posted at Malta were received on Monday from both the soldiers. Private Kaye's message bore the postmark August 8th, and read as follows:—

"Just a few lines to let you know that I am in the best of health. We arrived quite safe at Malta, and we have had a fine time. It is a fine place and the weather is splendid. There are all sorts of warships here. We are expecting to stay about two days, and then another four days' sailing."

Private Kaye is 19 years of age and is the youngest son of Mr. and Mrs. Thomas Kaye. He

Private W. Hart.

all right. We are going to have about seven more days' sailing before we land at the Dardanelles."

Private Hart, who is the eldest son of Mrs. and the late Mr. William Hart, is 22 years of age. He enlisted on April 24th, and was previously employed by Messrs. Peter Walker and Son, Ltd. He is a member of the "Loyal Perseverance" Lodge of the National Independent Order of Oddfellows. He was educated at St. Ann's School.

It is understood that both soldiers are able to swim.

Private Thomas Kaye.

enlisted three months ago, and before setting sail for the Dardanelles came home on five days' leave. Before joining the Army he was employed as a moulder at the Grappenhall Works of the Richmond Gas Stove and Meter Co., Ltd. He was educated at St. Benedict's School and attended the Gospel Hall. His brother, Driver John Kaye, is with the R.F.A. at the Front.

Another cutting from the *Warrington Guardian*. Neither 'lad' survived. *Ros Pates*

Edward it is necessary to go back for over 20 years to the sinking of the *Kowshing* during the Chino-Japanese War. This vessel, which had left Taku with 1,200 Chinese troops and guns, as well as small arms and ammunition, on board, was sunk off Chomulpo by the Japanese cruiser *Naniwa*. Whether the ship was sunk by torpedo or gunfire is in doubt, but about a thousand of the Chinese soldiers were drowned. An idea of the magnitude of the Transport Service is afforded by Mr Churchill's statement that the Admiralty has on charter approximately one-fifth of the total British mercantile tonnage, or about 4,000,000 tons. It is pertinent to recall that while this task of transportation has been carried out under the protection of the Grand Fleet in the North Sea, and has been conducted by naval convoys, it is the Mercantile Marine upon which has devolved the actual business of the undertaking. Hitherto, beyond the public acknowledgement which Mr Churchill made in February in the House of Commons, no official recognition has been made of the great service which has been rendered in connection with the progress of the war.'

* * *

Scotsman A. T. Fraser, a soldier with the Border Regiment, was in a deckchair on the afterdeck starboard side when suddenly dozens of men ran past him from port to starboard. The explosion came before he had time to ask what was the matter.

'The ship had no escort and we had not been ordered to have our lifebelts with us. The hundreds on deck ran below to get their lifebelts and hundreds below that would have met them on their way up. I shared a cabin accessible from the deck I was on and I raced there to get my lifebelt and ran to my lifeboat station, which was on the starboard side. As the men arrived they fell in two ranks. Already the ship was listing and this prevented our boats from being lowered, so we were ordered to jump for it. I saw no panic, but of course one could imagine what was happening on the inside stairs. I swam away from the ship and turned to see the funnels leaning towards me. When they reached the sea, all the soot was belched out, there was a loud whoosh and the ship sank. No explosion, no surge. So I was alone. The little waves were such that in the trough you saw nothing, on the crest you saw a few yards. The water was warm. I wondered if there were sharks.'

Fraser found some wood to rest on and a seaman, an older man who had twice previously been torpedoed, joined him. This brought the young Scot confidence. An up-turned *Royal Edward* lifeboat was to provide 17 of the survivors with a little more security, although in what Fraser calls half-hourly recurring turbulence, the boat turned over, offering them conventional but completely waterlogged accommodation every alternate half hour, but at least providing them with something to do. There was no singing and little conversation.

The first ship that passed hailed the scattered men and promised to signal for help – it could not stop as it had high explosives for Lemnos. Some of the men became depressed and showed unwillingness to clamber back into the lifeboat when it overturned, but on each occasion all were persuaded. Finally the hospital ship *Soudan* arrived to pick them up in her lifeboats, and at 2 o'clock Fraser was safely aboard, after just under 5 hours in the sea. He remembers that a large number of men lost their false teeth as they were constantly sick in the sea, and those men were sent back to England. 'We, the younger ones, were clothed and kitted and on another ship three days later for Gallipoli.'

* * *

20637 Lance Corporal Edward James Tuttle, 1st Battalion Essex Regiment, was one of those to die that morning. (The date given in *History of the Norfolk Regiment* was 14 August and the date on the back of the photograph of him, written by his mother, says 15 August, but the Essex Museum confirms 13 August as being the correct date.) He was aged 20 years and has no known grave. He is remembered on the Cape Helles Memorial, Gallipoli, Turkey, panel No 229-233 (Royal British Legion), and also in Mattishall Church. The Special Provisions Act 1957 Death Certificate has him listed as 'Private Tuttle, Edward James, age 20, England, 13.8.1915, at sea, drowned'.

One of the features of the Cape Helles monument is the rows of names of men drowned in the torpedoing of the *Royal Edward*. On Remembrance Sunday in 1989, a wreath of poppies was placed at the base of the Memorial, the message reading: 'In fond remembrance of a brave young soldier. It took us three years but we are so

Lance Corporal Edward James Tuttle, 1st Battalion Essex Regiment, commemorated on the Cape Helles Memorial. *Pauline Dodd*

pleased we found your last resting-place, Teddie. Pauline and John' (Teddie's sister and brother).

* * *

Nineteen-year-old Northampton man, Myles Darbyshire, says that it was a calm sea when the torpedo struck. Myles was among the reinforcements on the *Royal Edward* being sent to help the 29th Division in Gallipoli, and was a stretcher-bearer with the Lancashire Field Ambulance. He says that a group of them were in a lifeboat for the best part of a day after the ship went down. Stripped almost naked, they were roasted in the intense heat from the Aegean summer sun in a cloudless sky and from the hot wind. They were eventually spotted and rescued by one of the hospital ships, most likely the *Soudan*. He said, when recalling the whole experience, that he sees that ship going down every night – that it is one of those experiences one can never forget. Myles was one of the lucky few. He went on to have a long life in Northampton, eventually retiring in the middle of the 20th century as a District Road Motor Engineer with British Rail.

* * *

A further account of the sinking is provided by Sir Julian Corbett's *History of the Great War: Naval Operations, Volume 11* (Longmans Green & Company, London, 1940):

'Hitherto the anti-submarine organisation in the Aegean had seemed to be all that was required, but on August 13th the *Royal Edward*, a transport of some 11,000 tons, carrying drafts from Egypt for the XXIXth Division and other details to the number of nearly 1,400 officers and men, was torpedoed just as she was approaching Kandhelioussa island, off the Gulf of Kos. It was a landfall on the direct route into the Aegean from Alexandria, which the transports for Mudros

were still taking, and was in the patrol area assigned to the French. It would appear that the German submarine *UB14*, one of the new small class that had been brought overland to the Adriatic in sections, had put into the Gulf of Kos on her way from Cattero to the Bosporus in order to operate against the transport line. Her lurking place was in a lonely little cove called Orak Bay, ten miles east of Bodrum, in the vicinity of which we had long suspected that a submarine base had been established, but whether or not it had existed it had never been discovered. As soon as the loss was known two French destroyers were ordered to the spot; the hospital ship *Soudan* was also there and a trawler or two. One of the rescue ships that day was the *Achilles*, which rescued 29 survivors. However, between them and despite their best efforts, they saved less than 500 souls.'

* * *

The Gallipoli War Diary of Second Lieutenant John Lilingston-Reid (1886-1958), 1st/2nd County of London Yeomanry, Westminster Dragoons, 2nd Mounted Division, under Major-General W. E. Peyton CB, 5th Brigade, also records the sinking:

'14th August 1915
Left Cairo at 2.30am from Abassisa station. General Maxwell present to see us off. Arrive Alexandria 8.30am and embark on *Caledonia* for Mudros leaving at 6pm.

The Regiment goes out dismounted and numbers 350 men. I am given a troop in Major Morrison Bell's squadron, none of whom I know by name & most of them I have never seen before.

15th August 1915
Beautiful calm passage on very comfortable boat. Message comes in by Marconi that the

Royal Edward troopship in front of us has been torpedoed. About 400 lives saved out of 1300 men. We change our course.'

* * *

Together with the many hundreds lost from the sinking of the *Royal Edward* was a recipient of the Victoria Cross, Major Cuthbert Bromley of the 1st Lancashire Fusiliers, son of the late Sir John Bromley CB and Lady Bromley, of Sutton Corner, Seaford, Sussex. His Victoria Cross citation from the London Gazette of 15 March 1917 read:

'On the 25th April, 1915, headquarters and three companies of the 1st Battalion, Lancashire Fusiliers, in effecting a landing on the Gallipoli Peninsula to the West of Cape Helles, were met by very deadly fire from hidden machine-guns, which caused a great number of casualties. The survivors, however, rushed up to and cut the wire entanglements, notwithstanding the terrific fire from the enemy, and after overcoming supreme difficulties, the cliffs were gained and the position maintained. Amongst the many very gallant officers and men engaged in this most hazardous undertaking, Captain Bromley, Serjeant Stubbs, and Corporal Grimshaw have been selected by their comrades as having performed the most single acts of bravery and devotion to duty.'

At dawn on 25 April the 1st Battalion, Lancashire Fusiliers, part of the British 29th Division, had landed on W Beach, to the west of Cape Helles, the southernmost tip of the Gallipoli Peninsula. The Turks waited until the Fusiliers were almost ashore then opened fire.

Despite heavy losses the Fusiliers had kept a toehold on the beach and eventually advanced up both sides of the cliff, driving the defending Turks out of their trenches. Later that morning other

Cuthbert Bromley VC, remembered on the Helles Memorial. Here too the date of the sinking is incorrect. *James Fanning*

units were diverted to W Beach to reinforce the troops who were advancing on their inland objectives.

Six VCs were eventually awarded for this action, and W Beach was renamed 'Lancashire Landing' in honour of the Battalion that had captured it.

* * *

Another witness account came from a prominent and highly decorated nurse, Katy Beaufoy. This remarkable lady had kept a detailed war diary from May 1915 when she left Devonport on the RMS *Orsova*. Because the diary contained sensitive military information she did not post it but left each instalment with her family in Birmingham whenever she returned on leave. Here is her entry for the day that the *Royal Edward* sank:

'13th August 1915
We were told that we must go out the same evening, but about 8 or 8.30 the *Royal Edward*, who took our berth in Alexandria to embark troops and follow us up, was torpedoed by submarine just outside the harbour. 1,100 troops and about 400 crew; a few hundred only saved. A destroyer rushed out to rescue them, having received the

distress SOS signals. There have been about 10,000 casualties this last week, one boat took 1,100 another 1,800. The HMS *Doris* hit pretty badly, lost 2 guns, not sure about loss of life, hope none of our friends are lost – nothing much gained as yet at the Dardanelles – a fresh landing certainly but naught else, it is fearful. The E Lancs and Manchesters got between 2 hills and were completely wiped out. Two new sisters came from the Simla at 11.30pm, B. Henderson SN and S. A. O'Riordan SN.'

Sadly, Miss Beaufoy was herself the victim of a torpedo in 1918, as described in her obituary in *The Birmingham Weekly Post* of Saturday 9 March 1918:

'Miss Katy Beaufoy, the matron on the torpedoed hospital ship, *Glenart Castle*, was a Birmingham lady and it is feared she is among the missing. She was a daughter of the late Mr Thomas Beaufoy, for many years an official of the Birmingham Post Office, and a sister of Mrs J. Howard Kirk, of The Grange, Shirley, where she made her home.

Miss Beaufoy was matron of the Military Hospital at Exeter when the South African war broke out, and she volunteered for active service, and served throughout the war. For three years she was assistant matron of the Queen of Italy's Polytechnic in Rome, for the training of young Italian nurses, for which she was decorated. Miss Beaufoy volunteered immediately the present war broke out, and for the early months of the war was at Devonport Military Hospital. From there she was sent to Ras-el-Din Hospital at Alexandria. She had her first ship, the *Ionian*, at Mudros, after which she was appointed matron of the New Khedivial Hotel at Alexandria.

In June 1916 she was appointed matron of the *Dover Castle*, in which she continued for 15 months, only being absent for a few days when the vessel was torpedoed in the Mediterranean. After being on shore for a short time she was given the *Glenart Castle* on her first voyage, from November to February, and was in her when she was torpedoed on 26 February.'

* * *

A Kettering man, Charles William Ward, was already in his late 40s when the First World War broke out and therefore too old to go to the front. However, he joined the war effort as an ambulance attendant with the Royal Army Medical Corps, and on 13 August 1915 found himself heading for the Dardanelles aboard the *Royal Edward* to attend to any casualties.

He remembered that it was a sunny Friday morning when the torpedo struck. He was sucked under the water but was pulled to safety, barely conscious, by a man who was also from Kettering and who managed to get him to a lifeboat. Sadly, the effort of all this was too much for his rescuer, and he died from the exertion. Charles never forgot this act of bravery, and also the fact that his life had been saved by such a strong swimmer *from Kettering*! As a result he donated the Royal Edward Works Cup, to be competed for annually by teams from Kettering firms. His idea was to encourage interest in swimming, knowing that it had saved his life and could save others. The cup was first presented in 1922, and was well supported, becoming a major feature of the annual gala.

Charles lived until he was 91 years old and every night until his death he said he used to wake with nightmares about the torpedo explosion.

By 1983 only two teams were competing for the swimming trophy. I spoke with the chair of the Kettering Swimming Club, John Harris, and president Don Ward, and it would appear that the Cup was last won by the Kettering Leisure Village at a time when it was experiencing financial difficulties. The Cup had been placed in a secure 'lock-up' and has since mysteriously disappeared. Its insured value was in the region of £3,000, although the insurance company failed to pay out.

Having been born in Kettering myself, I find it somewhat eerie that after all this investigation into the *Royal Edward* at least two of her passengers that day should have been from my part of the world. But there was much more to this Kettering connection, hitherto unreported since 1915. To illustrate this book I needed to have a photograph of the Royal Edward Works Cup, so I spoke to a fellow journalist, Paul Whitelam, at the Kettering *Evening Telegraph*. Paul said he would do his best to issue an appeal in the form of a small article. I gave him a few basic details on the phone and sent a picture of the *Royal Edward* by email, and an article headlined 'Torpedoed – but not forgotten' was published in May 2003.

I wasn't sure if anything would come from the piece, but I thought it was certainly worth a shot,

especially if just one person could supply me with a picture of the elusive Cup. Sure enough, within two days of its publication a message was left for me at the office that a lady from Kettering had called after reading the article, and would I please get in touch.

She told me to speak up, as she was a tad hard of hearing. 'Yes,' she said when I asked her, rather loudly, if she had a photograph of the trophy. Her late husband had worked for the Kaycee clothing factory in Kettering, which had closed in April 1975, and had competed for the Cup on many occasions as part of the firm's swimming relay team. We arranged that I should call to see her and collect a picture for use in the book. It felt quite strange to be looking at an old black and white

The victorious Kaycee factory swimming team in 1962. They were regular winners of the Royal Edward Works Cup, donated by *Royal Edward* survivor Charles William Ward. Left to right, they are Len Holland, Ray Jones, Norman Coles and Charles Jacques. *Joyce Jacques*

KETTERING MEN

ON BOARD THE ILL-FATED ROYAL EDWARD.

AMBULANCE MEN'S UNKNOWN FATE.

A KETTERING QUARTERMASTER-SERGEANT RESCUED.

There is every reason to fear that at least ten men from the Kettering district were on the British transport Royal Edward, which was sunk by an enemy submarine in the Ægean Sea on Saturday morning.

The details of the Royal Army Medical Corps on board the Royal Edward included nine ambulance men from the Kettering district, who left Kettering in February last for Ipswich, where they have been serving in the Royal Army Medical Corps previous to being drafted to the Dardanelles.

They comprised Ptes. C. W. Ward, W. H. Bates, E. W. Toseland, R. W. Walker, J. C. Howard, E. Hughes, J. Summerfield (Kettering), H. Wills (Walgrave), Z. Bailey (Grafton Underwood). Pte. T. Dyson also left Kettering with the same party, but owing to trouble with his arm due to vaccination was unable to accompany his comrades on the Royal Edward, which sailed on July 30th.

LOSS OF KETTERING MEN CONFIRMED.

On Thursday morning Mr. Hy. Raby, superintendent of the St. John Ambulance Brigade, Kettering, received an official intimation from the War Office to the effect that Privates W. H. Bates, J. C. Howard, E. Hughes, and E. W. Toseland, all of Kettering, and among the R.A.M.C. members on board the ill-fated Royal Edward, had been reported as "missing, supposed drowned." The letter also expressed deep sympathy with the bereaved relatives.

It is known that Ptes. Waller, Ward, and Bailey were saved. Two others, Ptes. Summerfield and Herbert Wills, have not yet been accounted for, and Supt. Raby has received no reply with regard to these, but it is believed they were on the boat with the others. Pte. Dyson, it will be remembered, was not allowed to go with them on account of illness.

Ptes. Hughes, Howard, and Bates passed the first-aid examination in December, 1913, and Bates also gained the nursing certificate. Pte. Toseland passed the first-aid in October, 1914, and secured the nursing certificate in December. The four who are missing were all well known and esteemed young men and natives of the town. They all took the first opportunity that presented itself of joining the R.A.M.C. at Ipswich. Supt. Raby has been in possession of certificates for Ptes. Wills, Bates, and Toseland, which would have been presented to them on their return. Each was signed by Dr. Audland.

NAVAL DISASTER.

British Transport Sunk by Submarine.

HEAVY LOSS OF LIFE IN THE ÆGEAN.

Press Bureau,
Tuesday 12.40 p.m.

The Secretary of the Admiralty issued the following:—

The British transport Royal Edward was sunk by an enemy submarine in the Ægean Sea last Saturday morning.

According to the information at present available the transport had on board 32 military officers and 1,350 troops, in addition to the ship's crew of 220 officers and men. The troops consisted mainly of reinforcements for the 29th Division, and details of the R.A.M.C.

Above A report from the Kettering *Evening Telegraph* on 17 August 1915.

Top left News comes in that men from Kettering are involved in the tragedy, 18 August 1915.

Left Grim confirmation that Kettering men had lost their lives, 3 September 1915. *All Frank Foulds* picture from the 1960s of four men collecting a trophy that had been named in honour of one Kettering man saving another on the morning that the *Royal Edward* had sunk all those years ago. I must confess that I had a tear in my eye when I first saw the image.

The whole Kettering connection was breathtaking enough, but I was in for an even greater surprise the following morning. Another message was waiting for me to call a lady in Burton Latimer who had also seen the article and who also had information regarding the *Royal Edward.* I wondered what this could possibly be – perhaps someone else with a photograph of the Works Cup.

Imagine my surprise to learn that there were more than two Kettering men on the *Royal Edward* that morning in the Aegean. A total of ten men from Kettering's St John Ambulance Brigade had all headed for, and signed up in, Suffolk to be a part of the medical contingent that would head for the Aegean aboard the *Royal Edward.* They had all joined the Royal Army Medical Corps, which, at that time, was screaming for volunteers to tend the wounded on the battlefields of Gallipoli.

Our ten intrepid Kettering lads left Kettering for Ipswich in February 1915, to be 'processed' through the East Anglian Casualty Clearing Station. All ten were sent on to Watford for two weeks of further training in the Royal Army Medical Corps, and eventually were despatched to Avonmouth to join HMT *Royal Edward*, which would convey them to the theatre of war.

Following the disaster the local newspaper initially reported that a major sea tragedy had occurred, then that there might have been some men from Kettering on board. Finally, it confirmed the grim news of the loss that would be felt by the whole Kettering community.

Once again, it seemed so strange to me that a tale which had begun because of my curiosity about a young man from Scotland joining the Canadian Mercantile Marine and going off to sea as a merchantman on an ocean-going liner, should now find focus in the very town in which I was born.

Throughout Britain there are hundreds of people who are related to all of those killed on the *Royal Edward,* and for every one that died and survived there is undoubtedly a tale to be told. I am most surprised at my own family's lack of remembrance with regard to William, and that I had to scurry around for snippets of information – that I had a problem finding even a half-decent picture of a man who was obviously sufficiently well self-educated, motivated and determined, at such a tender age, to make his mark and to discover the world, even before the outbreak of hostilities. One would think that every member of my family would have been aware of William's complete story. But no. Sadly, there are even some who are still unaware of his very existence.

Of the ten Kettering men who set out for Avonmouth, just four survived. The six that perished were John Howard, Ernest Toseland, Ernest Hughes, William Harry Bates, James Summerfield and Herbert Wills. The four survivors were Charles William Ward, R. W. Waller, Zachariah Bailey and T. Dyson. Zac Bailey had been hanging out his washing when the torpedo struck and was thrown clear of the ship; later a cablegram was received at his Grafton Underwood home to say that he was safe. Another of the survivors, Private Waller, had sent a letter home dated 30 July that simply stated: 'I have embarked on the *Royal Edward.*' In a later letter to his wife, dated 2 August, and probably posted later in Malta, he said that they were having a 'fine journey'. T. Dyson made it to Avonmouth but was refused boarding due to illness. An inoculation had reacted badly and he was deemed unfit for service on that occasion.

Three days after the *Royal Edward* had sunk, the caretaker of Rockingham Road School in Kettering, Walter Toseland, received a letter from his son Ernest that had been posted when the ship had arrived at Malta on 6 August:

The *Royal Edward*'s 'Kettering Boys': (back row) James Summerfield, Zachariah (Zac) Bailey of Grafton Underwood. R. W. Waller of Hawthorn Road, Kettering, T. Dyson, John Charles Tyrrell Howard of 42 Lindsay Street, Kettering, and Ernest Walter Toseland of School House, Dryden Street, Kettering; (front row) Ernest Hughes of 247 Havelock Street, Kettering, Herbert Wills of Walgrave, Charles William Ward, and William Henry (Harry) Bates of 122 Bath Road, Kettering. *Frank Foulds*

'I must say we have had a very nice voyage so far, although I was a bit seedy going through the Bay of Biscay. We are on one of the Canadian boats called the *Royal Edward* and it is rather a large one. It is simply lovely going along the Mediterranean Sea, as it is very clear and such a lovely colour, and we can just see the hills of Africa in the distance.'

On Sunday 3 October 1915 a memorial service was held at Kettering's St Andrew's Church for all the men who had lost their lives in the tragedy. The service began at 3pm and was conducted by the Chaplain Reverend F. H. Lang, Rector of nearby Twywell.

The men of Kettering are remembered today on the town's cenotaph to the Glorious Dead, and on the Helles memorial on the Gallipoli peninsula. Perhaps it is just a sign of the times, or maybe I'm missing something, but as I was preparing to take a few pictures of the Kettering memorial I needed to ask some youths if they would kindly move to allow a clear picture. They were using the memorial for skateboard practice, and it saddened me.

A soldier from Kettering also survived. Mrs Tingle of 13 Argyll Street, Kettering, was sitting at home as the news of the *Royal Edward* began to filter through. Men from all over had been heading in the direction of Gallipoli and she knew that there was a chance that her husband may have been

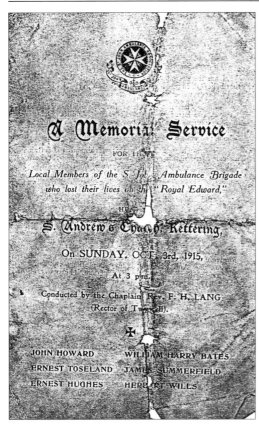

Above The order of service for the Memorial Service to the six Kettering men lost on board the *Royal Edward*. *Janet Peck*

Above right Ernest Toseland. *Janet Peck*

Right Four of the six men of Kettering who lost their lives on HMT *Royal Edward* are remembered on the town's memorial to the Glorious Dead. *Author*

aboard the ill-fated ship. Quartermaster-Sergeant Tingle of the 1/4th Northamptonshire Battalion, part of the East Midlands Brigade, East Anglian Division, had indeed boarded the *Royal Edward*. He was employed as a clerk by the Kettering firm of Wallis & Linnell and was also in the Territorial Army, which had been mobilised that July and August. Happily, only four days after the sinking, at 10 o'clock in the morning his wife received a cablegram that had been handed in at 9.05pm of 16 August and sent to her via Alexandria. It read simply: 'Safe – Tingle.' One can only assume that he had been plucked from the Aegean by one of the rescue ships and had been dropped off safely in the *Royal Edward*'s last port of call.

One published account says that some of his comrades had gone ahead on the *Royal George*, but he was part of what was called the Divisional Headquarters Staff, which all boarded the *Royal Edward* the following day. What is strange is that the Northamptonshire Battalion was part of what became the 162nd Brigade, the 54th East Anglian Division, whose published details of events from August 1915 make no mention of the *Royal Edward*, the *Royal George* or Avonmouth. Indeed, in its Synopsis of the history of the Division, it clearly states that in July 1915 they all embarked at Liverpool for Mudros. Therefore the question remains – why was Quartermaster-Sergeant Tingle aboard the *Royal Edward*, and (by other accounts) not with the rest of his comrades boarding at Liverpool?

* * *

My Great Uncle Willie is listed as a 5th Engineering Officer in the Canadian Mercantile Marine, and would probably have been one of 10 to 15 engineers, depending on the size of the ship and/or the horsepower of the main engines. He would have been the second of three or four watch-keeping engineers in the 4-8 watch (0400-1800 and 1600-2000) under the Second Engineer as senior watch-keeper. He may well have been the engineer keeping watch in the boiler-room as opposed to the main engine-room, if the ship was a steamship, which, of course, the *Royal Edward* was. As well as his watch-keeping duties he would also have been involved in any routine and breakdown maintenance and upkeep of the machinery.

His uniform would have been in the traditional Navy-style double breasted blue with either company livery or standard Merchant Navy buttons (eight) and insignia. The insignia of rank

for a Fifth Engineer would have been one ¼-inch stripe on each cuff with a purple narrow band below. If he held a Certificate of Competency the stripe would also include a diamond. The salary scale in 1915 would equate to £18,000 today.

Given the facts of the event and the eye-witness accounts of survivors, it can fairly safely be assumed that William would have been at his post, in the boiler-room, that morning when the torpedo struck. With the decks packed to the gunnels with troops and with space being at such a premium, those on board serving with the Canadian Mercantile Marine would have been all too busy at their allotted duties.

It is also logical to assume that anyone working in William's environment would not have had time to even make it to daylight in only 6 minutes. The stern of the ship would have been blown apart. According to another first-hand account, only seven of the 33 lifeboats had time to get clear of the ship. It all happened so quickly. Great Uncle Willie was just 25.

His parents would have received the tragic news at their home at 58 Church Street in Coatbridge. It was said that his mother had had a premonition, and already knew of Willie's death. Indeed, it was she who had written the poem of remembrance that appeared in the local newspaper alongside his photograph – and had written it *before* receiving the news.

His message

At my post, dear mother mine,
I have reached the shore divine,
God has answered clear your prayer,
He has kept me ever near.

What I've failed in, He'll forgive,
God in Heaven doth ever live,
Keep on praying mother dear,
He will answer every prayer.

William is remembered in his home town on the memorial at the corner of Blair Road in Coatbridge.
Author

Honour bright has been my aim,
I have never sought for fame,
Only answered duty's call,
Reach the everlasting goal.

Now dear mother, weep no more,
Since I've reached the Golden Shore;
God you trust, he'll never fail,
Till you're safe inside the veil.

'Look to Jesus'

Our Willie is remembered by the people of his town together with all of the fallen from the Great War. His name – 'NIMMO WM. D. D. 2nd LT. RN' – is listed on the Coatbridge memorial to the dead, an imposing monument standing next to the busy western approach to the town. It was designed by Edith Burnet Hughes (1888-1971) and erected in 1926. She was the first female architect in Scotland, trained at Aberdeen School of Art from 1915 (ironically) to 1925, and later became an assistant lecturer at Aberdeen Technical College. She lived and died at Tirranmuir, Kippen, Stirlingshire.

I ran my fingers along William's name and shed a tear for a man I had never met. This had been my first 'tangible' contact.

His name also appears on the Tower Hill Memorial in London, commemorating men of the Merchant Navy and fishing fleets who died in both World Wars and who have no known grave. It stands on the south side of the garden of Trinity Square, London, close to the Tower of London. In the First World War the civilian navy's duty was to be the supply service of the Royal Navy, to transport troops and supplies to the armies, to transport raw materials to overseas munitions factories and munitions from those factories, to maintain, on a reduced scale, the ordinary import and export trade, to supply food to the home country and – in spite of

greatly enlarged risks and responsibilities – to provide both personnel and ships to supplement the existing resources of the Royal Navy. Losses of men and vessels were high from the outset, but peaked in 1917 when in January the German Government announced the adoption of 'unrestricted submarine warfare'. The subsequent preventative measures introduced by the Ministry of Shipping – including the setting up of the convoy system where warships were used to escort merchant vessels – led to a decrease in losses, but by the end of the war 3,305 merchant ships had been lost with a total of 17,000 lives. The First World War section of the Tower Hill Memorial commemorates almost 12,000 seamen who have no grave but the sea.

The Tower Hill Memorial, London. *Frank McCormick*

The memorial was designed by Sir Edwin Lutyens with sculpture by Sir William Reid-Dick.

On seeing the structure for the first time I was immediately struck by its historic location. Directly opposite is one of London's most famous landmarks: the Tower of London. Millions of tourists must file past the memorial every year, many I suspect little realising the significance of what is behind them, as they take picture after picture of the famous tower. Indeed, why should they: these are happy days.

William's name, together with the other merchantmen that lost their lives that day, can be found in section 15 on the monument. The name *Royal Edward Toronto* is followed by her master's name, 'WOTTON P. M.'. Thereafter the names of her fallen crew are listed alphabetically. William is simply 'NIMMO W. D. D.'. When my wife and I visited the site on Saturday 24 August 2003 the brightness of the day made it difficult to photograph Willie's inscription. He is listed on the fifth panel from the bottom on the edge side of section 15. One would need a step-ladder to get a true face-on picture. As a compromise, Caroline used her video camera to get close-up shots of *all* the names, that they may be listed at the end of this book as a written memorial.

Yet again, much in the same way as I had felt when visiting the Coatbridge memorial, I was filled with sadness as I surveyed row upon row of young lives lost. And yet I felt a great closeness to my mother's uncle, just by seeing his name listed in front of my eyes.

On the Gallipoli peninsula itself the Helles Memorial serves the dual function of Commonwealth battle memorial for the whole Gallipoli campaign and a place of commemoration for many of those Commonwealth servicemen who died there and have no known grave. The

The Helles Memorial. *Paul Reed*

United Kingdom and Indian forces named on the memorial died in operations throughout the peninsula, the Australians at Helles. There are also panels for those who died or were buried at sea in Gallipoli waters. Designed by Sir John Burnet, the Helles Memorial was completed in 1924 and is built of rough stone from Ilgardere. It bears more than 21,000 names, the largest number from the Lancashire Fusiliers (1,357 commemorations) on panels 58-72, and the Manchester Regiment (1,215 commemorations) on panels 158-170. The memorial stands on the tip of the peninsula and is in the form of an obelisk more than 30 metres high, which can be seen by ships passing through the Dardanelles.

There are four other memorials to the missing at Gallipoli: The Lone Pine, Hill 60, and Chunuk Bair Memorials commemorate Australian and New Zealanders at Anzac, while the Twelve Tree Copse Memorial commemorates the New Zealanders at Helles. Naval casualties of the United Kingdom lost or buried at sea are recorded on their respective memorials at Portsmouth, Plymouth and Chatham.

* * *

The bronze Mercantile Marine War Medal was awarded to those who received the British War Medal and also served at sea on at least one voyage through a danger zone. The medal was also awarded to those who had served at sea for not less than six months between 4 August 1914 and 11 November 1918. The obverse bore the head of King George V, the reverse a merchant ship ploughing her way through stormy seas, an enemy submarine sinking and a sailing vessel in the background. Below, the inscription 'FOR * WAR * SERVICE / MERCANTILE MARINE / * 1914-1918 *' appears in three lines. Around the edge of the rim are raised laurel leaves. The ribbon is 1¼ inches wide and is coloured green and red separated by a thin white middle stripe,

representing starboard and port running lights with the masthead steaming light in the centre. Of a total of 133,135, 624 were issued to Canadians, and William would have been entitled to this medal posthumously.

The British War Medal was instituted to record the successful conclusion of the First World War, but was extended to cover the period 1919-20 and service in mine-clearing at sea as well as participation in operations in North and South Russia, the Eastern Baltic, Siberia, the Black Sea and the Caspian. It was originally intended to award campaign bars, but 79 were recommended by the Army and 68 by the Navy, so the scheme was abandoned as impractical. The Naval bars were actually authorised (7 July 1920) and miniatures are known with them, though the actual bars were never issued. A circular, silver medal, it was 1.42 inches in diameter (the medal awarded to Chinese, Maltese and native labour corps was bronze). The obverse again shows the King George V, in a profile by Sir Bertram Mackennal. On the reverse a horseman (St George, naked), armed with a short sword (an allegory of the physical and mental strength that achieved victory over Prussianism), tramples on the Prussian shield and the skull and cross-bones. Just off-centre, near the right upper rim, is the sun of Victory. The dates 1914 and 1918 appear in the left and right fields respectively. Some 6,500,000 were struck in silver and 110,000 in bronze (mainly for Chinese, Indian and Maltese personnel in labour battalions). The medal was authorised on 26 July 1919, and again William would have been entitled to this medal posthumously.

It remains a mystery as to the whereabouts of Great Uncle Willie's medals and ownership. However, indicative of how time and technology has moved on, he is remembered on the 'virtual' Canadian War Memorial on the internet. He was obviously a bright young man – I'm sure he would have approved.

* * *

And what of Heino Von Heimburg, who commanded *UB14* when she sank the *Royal Edward*? The submarine undertook 22 patrols from 1 July 1915 to 11 November 1918, either in the Pola Flotilla or the Constantinople Flotilla. In all she sank a total of 13,622 tons of Allied shipping, not including warships. She sank two British submarines, the *E7* and the *E20* in the Dardanelles and the Sea of Marmara respectively. She was eventually disarmed at Sevastopol on 25 November 1918 after surrendering in Malta. *UB14* was eventually broken up in 1920. But what of the man who had caught the *Royal Edward* in his sights?

One need only start with the question: which was the most successful submarine? The answer is, bizarrely enough, a German First World War submarine, the *U35*, which spent most of its career

Only 49 Pour le Mérite medals were given to German Navy personnel. The so-called 'Blue Max' was awarded to OberLt Heino von Heimburg of *UC-22* on 11 August 1917, just two years after the sinking of the *Royal Edward*.
H. V. Heimburg

operating out of Austrian ports. Under four distinguished commanders she would sink 224 merchant ships of 539,741 tons together with the sloop HMS *Primula*. These commanders were, in turn, Waldemar Kophamel, Lothar von Arnauld de la Periere, Ernst von Voigt, and Heino von Heimburg. Kophamel, von Arnauld de la Periere, and von Heimburg were three of the 29 German submarine commanders to be awarded the Pour le Mérite, though Kophamel and Heimburg received the award for service on other ships.

In the small German state of Brandenburg, the Ordre de la Générosité (Order of Generosity – French was the official language of the Prussian court at the time) was established by Friedrich Wilhelm I, the electoral prince, on 12 May 1667. On 6 June 1740 the decoration was renamed the Pour Le Mérite (For Merit) by Friedrich II, who was also known as Friedrich the Great. The new order was to serve as a reward to loyal subjects for meritorious service in the pending war over the territories of Silesia. However, it was during the Great War that the medal gained its fame. The creation of aerial combat brought forth a new breed of warrior who seemed glamorous and daring, and whose exploits were watched by thousands of soldiers down below in the trenches. In order for a pilot to be considered for the Pour Le Mérite, he would have to obtain a certain amount of aerial victories.

The first pilots to receive the award had to have eight aerial victories, and on 12 January 1916 Max Immelmann was the first to receive it; after that it became unofficially known as the 'Blue Max'. By January 1917 the requirements had been raised to 16 victories, and the only pilot to receive his award under those conditions was Manfred Freiherr Von Richthofen ('The Red Baron').

During the late 1800s it was the Kaiser's goal to build a strong Navy. Germany needed these ships to protect her colonies, so she began building a reputable fleet. This was the first time anyone came close to the rapid shipbuilding that Great Britain undertook. Shipping competition between the nations blossomed in the private ocean liner business during this time, especially during the early 1900s. The Kaiser prized this Navy very highly, so, when war broke out, he was hesitant to put up his fleet against the numerous British fleet; it was decided that the use of U-boats would be the course of action when it came to battle on the seas. This limited use of the Navy is the reason why only 49 Pour le Mérite awards were handed out to Navy personnel.

It is therefore no surprise that the first naval recipient of the Pour le Mérite was a U-boat commander, Kapitanleutnant Otto Weddigen from Saxony. Unfortunately, Weddigen died in battle before he could fully enjoy his award. The next recipient would be Kapitanleutnant Otto Hersing, who would actually have the chance to enjoy the fame and honour he received.

As for the higher-ranking recipients, the first to receive the Pour le Mérite was Grand Admiral Alfred von Tirpitz, the father of the modern German Navy. According to Admiral von Muller's diary, Tirpitz was given his award after the non-naval von Hohenborn received the decoration without much reason. Tirpitz had spent most of his life dedicated to the Navy and was dismayed at the lack of appreciation for his work; apparently he had even threatened several times to resign if he didn't have things his way. He was tired of seeing his fleet sit restless in German harbours while the German Army mobilised and fought every day.

Some of these naval awards seemed to be measured in part by tonnage of destroyed enemy vessels, as with the number of victories won by pilots. Though this did not seem to be the only means of measuring a candidate's worth, it must have helped in the selection process.

'Oakleaves' were originally established for the Red Eagle Order as an additional level to the order. The same was applied to the Pour Le Mérite on 10 March 1813. This special higher level was to be awarded for extraordinary achievements. No one in the air service received Oakleaves, even though Manfred Von Richthofen was considered for the award. It was to General Ludendorff's surprise that he did not receive the award.

Heino Von Heimburg was born in Hanover on 24 October 1889, frighteningly and coincidentally one month *exactly* before William. He entered the Navy on 3 April 1907, the year that the *Cairo* (*Royal Edward*) was launched, and rose to be a Vice-Admiral in the German fleet on 1 April 1942. He ended his days in captivity in a Russian prisoner of war camp near Stalingrad, and died as Vice-Admiral Heino Von Heimburg in 1945.

His grandson, also named Heino J. Von Heimburg, kindly supplied his grandfather's details and picture for use in this book.

6
Acts of Remembrance

On Tuesday 7 September 1915 *The Times* carried an article headed 'Memorial at Sea':

'SERVICE WHERE
THE *ROYAL EDWARD* SANK

We have received from the Rev Basil K. Bond, Chaplain to the Forces, who is attached to the hospital ship *Devanha*, an account of one of the most impressive funeral services of the war. Three weeks ago the country was told of the sinking of the transport *Royal Edward* in the Aegean Sea, with a thousand of the men she carried. Even before the news of the disaster was published here, a memorial service was held over the spot where the ship went down, and the bodies of those who had lost their lives were solemnly committed to the keeping of the sea. "It is our hope," writes the chaplain, "that the thought that such a service was held may give some comfort to the bereaved at home."

The *Royal Edward* was sunk a few minutes after 9 o'clock on the morning of Friday, August 13. The news quickly reached Alexandria, where the hospital ship *Devanha* was getting ready to sail, and at the suggestion of the captain it was arranged that a memorial service should be held at the scene of the disaster. The *Devanha* left Alexandria, and on the following evening those on board knew that they were nearing the spot, for lifeboats, lifebelts, soldiers' water bottles, planks, and other pieces of wreckage were seen floating on the water. Soon after half past 8 they came close upon the place, and the ship's bell tolled slowly while the Europeans in the ship assembled on the boatdeck to pay the last tribute to the dead. All were there – the captain, officers, engineers and stewards, the doctors, nurses, orderlies, and some of the men of the Royal Army Medical Corps who were passengers.

The service began with the hymn "Let Saints on earth in concert sing". Then came the opening sentences of the Burial Service, followed by the 46th Psalm – "God is our help and strength". During the singing of the Psalm the vessel slowed down until it stopped right over the place where the *Royal Edward* lay. The lesson was read, and the committal prayer for those buried at sea followed. The collect for All Saints Day, the prayer for those in anxiety and sorrow, and the prayer for our soldiers and sailors were offered. Then, as the ship gradually proceeded on her way, the blessing was given, and the hymn "Now the labourer's task is o'er" was sung. The National Anthem and the Dead March in *Saul* brought the service to an end.'

The SS (HMT) *Devanha. Bill Hutton*

The SS (HMT) *Devanha* was built in 1905/6 by Caird & Co, Greenock, Glasgow, for the P&O Line. She was a ship of 8,092 gross tons with an overall length of 470 feet and a beam of 56½ feet. She had one funnel, two masts, twin screws and a maximum speed of 15 knots. There was accommodation for 160 First and 80 Second Class passengers. Newly registered on 31 January 1906, she was placed on the UK to India and the Far East intermediate service. Used as a troop and hospital ship during the First World War, she landed the 12th Australian Battalion at Anzac Beach, Gallipoli, and remained there as a hospital ship with her sister ship *Dongola*. She was the last vessel to leave the beach area. On 5 April 1916 she picked up survivors from the torpedoed British India Line ship *Chantala* and landed them at Malta. From 1919 she returned to the Far East run with occasional voyages to Australia, and in March 1928 was sold for scrap and broken up in Japan.

Following in the wake of the disaster reports and diary entries were being made and found with regard to the affairs of the *Royal Edward*. One such account, somewhat ironic and yet humorous in its delivery, was published in *Stand To!*, the journal of the Western Front Association, in September 2002, No 65, by Paul Guthrie and Paul Bennett. The diary belonged to a young American, Frank Matthew Coffee, who died on 18 November 1915, well before the United States entered the war, while serving as a Lieutenant with the 24th Battalion, Australian Imperial Forces, in Gallipoli. How did this young Kentuckian die in a foreign army and foreign land? Well, that's another tale for others to tell.

'September 10th 1915

Half an hour ago we passed over the spot where the *Royal Edward* was submarined. One officer aboard, a South Wales Borderer, was saved from the *Royal Edward*. He was five hours in the water, being picked up by a French destroyer. The French officers did everything for him, brandy, rubbing and everything. He was just beginning to feel

Lieutenant Frank Matthew Coffee, 24th Battalion,
Australian Imperial Force. *Anzacs.org*

okay again when a British cruiser sent an
officer to see him.

The Navy Johnny wore a monocle, and this
was his greeting to a man just rescued: "Haw!
Have you a roll of those who were saved? Ba
Jove! What, you haven't? How extraordinary!
Good day, Sir!" Not a word of sympathy, but
the patient nearly laughed himself sick.
Picture a man clothed in a lifebelt calling the
roll of those afloat!'

Following the Great War members of the Kettering
Ambulance Brigade visited Northamptonshire's
ancient Rockingham Castle near Corby, just a
stone's throw from where I currently live in
Gretton. This was quite an event, with a parade,
demonstrations and presentations. The event was
reported in the local press on Friday 12 September
1919, having taken place on the previous Sunday,

the 7th. One of those attending was Private R. W.
Waller, one of the three men from Kettering who
had survived the *Royal Edward* sinking four years
earlier. 'Private Waller,' the paper reported, 'a
member of the party, recounted vividly several
incidents of the voyage of the *Royal Edward*, which
was torpedoed in the Aegean Sea.'

It wasn't long before visitors began arriving at
the cemeteries of Gallipoli. One Australian father
managed to reach Gallipoli in April 1920, where
the work of the Imperial War Graves Commission
was in full swing. In 1924 the Australian Prime
Minister, Stanley Melbourne Bruce, visited. In
1925 the liner *Ormonde* brought the New
Zealand High Commissioner to London and 400
others to unveil the New Zealand Memorial on
Chunuk Bair, and in 1935 General Sir William
Birdwood, the Anzac Corps commander in 1915,
walked again on the sand of Anzac Cove. Those
who visited in those early days after the Great
War were usually relatives of the dead with a
strong personal need to see the grave or
commemorated name of a loved one. Some of the
emotion they must have felt is conveyed in this
passage describing the arrival of the cruise ship
Duchess of Richmond at the Dardanelles in April
1934:

'In the quietude of the Aegean evening a
white-haired lady accompanied by a chaplain
walked slowly to the stern-rail of the *Duchess
of Richmond*, which was passing between the
islands. Almost unnoticed by anyone on
board, the padre offered a prayer and the lady
dropped a wreath upon the sea, for it was near
this spot where the transport *Royal Edward*,
conveying 1,400 troops, was lost in August
1915. Among the hundreds of young men
who went to their death in that swift tragedy
had been her only son.'

Kettering Ambulance Brigade at Rockingham Castle.

Practical Demonstration in Historic Grounds.

Guardian TWO CHURCH PARADES. *Sept 12 1917*

The Kettering Headquarters Division of the St. John Ambulance Brigade had a busy day on Sunday, when, at the kind invitation of the Rev. and Mrs. Wentworth Watson, of Rockingham Castle, they visited Rockingham. They paraded under the charge of Corps Supt. H. Raby at 9 a.m., and at 9.30 left for Rockingham, some travelling by cycle, some by char-a-banc, and others in the motor ambulance. They

seconded by Ambulance Officer W. Dyson. Mrs. Watson, in acknowledging the vote, extended a hearty invitation to the Brigade to hold their next annual camp at Rockingham, and promised to do all in her power to make the facilities adequate and enjoyable. The Brigade were then inspected by Mr. and Mrs. Watson, and they chatted interestedly with those members who had been on active service during the

Top row: Privates F. A. Loasby, W. R. Waller, W. Hankin, W. Wills, F. Payne, W. Hewitt, G. York, and H. Brook.
Second row: Privates T. L. Curtis, A. Coleman, W. Woolmer, G. Turner, M. Forster, W. Manville, A. Issitt, G. Sturman, W. Brown, and Sergt. J. Licquorice.
Bottom row: Staff-Sergt. J. Miller, Sgt. W. Groome, Supt. Chas. W. Curtis, Corps.-Supt. H. Raby, Ambulance Officer W. Dyson, Sergt. Tilley, and Staff-Sergt. Wilson.

paraded to Rockingham's pretty church on arrival, and subsequently had a full practice, including a sham railway accident. Luncheon was subsequently served at the Sondes Arms. In the afternoon they visited the beautiful grounds of the Castle, which were looking like the country round about, so well viewed from the magnificent terrace. After having had tea at the Sondes Arms, the Brigade paraded at the Castle, and

A PRESENTATION.

were cordially welcomed by the Rev. and Mrs. Wentworth Watson (the latter of whom, as is well - known, was actively associated during the war with the Kettering V.A.D at the Hospital, and evinced keen interest in ambulance work. Mrs. Watson kindly distributed a number of medallions and certificates, who was thanked by Supt. Raby,

war. Private Waller, a member of the party, recounted vividly several incidents of the voyage of the Royal Edward, which

Interested Spectators. was torpedoed in the

Aegean Sea. Later the Brigade paraded to church for evensong, after which the return journey to Kettering was made. The men were delighted with their experience, and appreciated to the full the cordiality of their welcome at the beautiful Rockingham Castle. There is little doubt that next year's annual camp will be held there. The sincerity of the invitation impressed every member of the Brigade.

Mrs. Wentworth Watson, Ambulance Officer. W. Dyson with a bronze label.

The Rev. Wentworth Watson and one of his house party watching Kettering Ambulance men at Rockingham Castle.

* * *

These days numerous diving schools operate along Turkey's coasts, particularly in the Aegean and the Mediterranean, and during the summer months perhaps a thousand people go diving each day.

In the North Aegean, however, mild temperatures for much of the year make it far easier for even fairly inexperienced divers to explore the large number of British, French and Italian ships sunk around Gallipoli and the Dardanelles during the First World War; over that period of nearly a year, several hundred ships and boats sank in the coastal waters between Anzac Cove and Suvla Bay on the western side of the peninsula. These included several warships, landing craft, and lighters carrying troops and provisions.

Today the locations of 216 of these wrecks have been identified, the most important being the British warships *Irresistible*, *Triumph*, *Ocean*, *Majestic* and *Goliath*, and the French *Bouvet*. Normally the boat ride takes just 20 minutes to an hour to reach the diving areas, so that two dives can be completed in a day. Of the ships that are at an accessible depth, one of the most important is the *Lundi*, which was sunk by torpedo on 15 April 1915. This wreck lies on sand at 27 metres in Suvla Bay, between the Büyük Kemikli and Küçük Kemikli headlands. Despite the intervening 81 years, this cargo ship, carrying supplies and ammunition, is largely intact and is home to a wide variety of marine life. The spaces between the sandy bottom and the ship's hull are a favourite haunt for lobsters and other crustaceans. On the deck just in front of the bridge is a colony of conger eels up to a metre in length. The hatch covers have rotted away, giving easy access to the hold towards the bow, and inside are shoals of bream and goby. The iron beams of the hold are covered with pink and yellow sponges, and the enclosed spaces are inhabited by corb fish (Corvina nigra).

The British warship HMS *Majestic* sank at right-angles to the shore in Morto Cove, so while its bow lies in 18 metres of water, its stern lies on sand at a depth of 29 metres. In the 1960s divers unfortunately dismantled the most interesting sections of the wreck, but the crow's nest can be seen lying 10 metres off. There is a cannon on the deck, which is so encrusted with barnacles that it has grown into the structure. Large numbers of bream, dentex and other fish frolic happily in the interior sections, which are inaccessible to divers.

A knowledge of lighters is useful for anyone investigating the wrecks round Gallipoli. These were sheet iron boats about 20 metres in length used by the British fleet to carry provisions and land troops between their base on Gökçeada (Imroz) and Gallipoli. Since they were open, many were sunk by gunfire or storms, and several are to be seen at depths of 28 to 30 metres. A lighter lying off Anzac Cove west of Kocatepe harbour is one of those most often visited by divers, both because it is within easy reach and because of its proximity to the other wrecks in Suvla Bay.

Two other lighters at a depth of 30 metres, and 15 metres apart, lying parallel to the southern shore of Morto Cove, provide interesting dives. One was carrying a wheeled steam boiler that now lies on its side in the sand on the port side of the bow. Shoals of liche (Turkish akya), a large, silver fish with a dark back often exceeding 1.5 metres in length, are one of the lighter wrecks' frequent inhabitants. These curious and lovely fish swim to meet divers and circle around them. They are sensitive to sound, and if divers tap their diving knives on metal as they swim, the liche will rush out to investigate the intruders.

Another interesting wreck is a steamship in Suvla Bay near Büyük Kemikli headland. Lying at 15 metres and largely buried under sand, the most notable feature of this wreck is its thickly armoured steam boiler, which exploded when the ship sank and broke into three sections. The proximity of this wreck to the shore in shallow water means that even inexperienced divers are able to explore it. The experience of witnessing historical evidence that divers alone can reach, combined with many varieties of marine creatures in their natural habitat, is a fascinating one, and brings both amateurs and professionals back to this area time after time.

Then there are the forgotten ships – the ships that went to the bottom in deep water – too deep for any diving expedition.

The *Royal Edward* has lain undisturbed on the ocean floor for nearly 90 years. The world it left behind was a very violent place at the start of a new century. It is here that hundreds of young people, my Great Uncle Willie included, lie in peace below the warm waters of the Aegean Sea. The captain of the ship – Commander Peter Wotton – the six men from Kettering, the ship's crew, Teddie Tuttle … they are all at rest where they fell in 1915.

It occurred to me that, at the time of writing, I had lived through 47 August the 13ths without realising any significance, and had decided that the 48th would be different. On 12 August 2003 I collected a beautiful yet modest flower arrangement from Cobby's florists in Northampton. Driving back to Gretton that afternoon my head was filled with conflicting ideas of how best to mark the following day's anniversary. Yet the best idea by far was simply to leave my small flower arrangement below the names of the Glorious Dead at the Kettering War Memorial in the centre of town. Therefore on the evening of the 12th (known in certain circles as the 'Glorious Twelfth', but for different reasons) I used my computer to create a page of text that would be attached to my tribute in a clear plastic sleeve:

'IN MEMORY OF ALL THOSE WHO LOST
THEIR LIVES WHEN
HMT *Royal Edward*
sank at a time of world conflict
Friday 13 August 1915 Aegean Sea
0800hrs

Seven men from Northamptonshire were among the one thousand remembered here today.
The Canadian Mercantile Mariners, all the soldiers and the medical staff. For all those who gave the ultimate sacrifice:
YOU MAY BE GONE, BUT YOU ARE *NEVER* FORGOTTEN!'

The following morning, despite temperatures well into the 80s yet again, I decided to wear a suit and tie as a mark of respect for the laying of my flowers. Thus at 9 o'clock on Wednesday 13 August 2003, almost exactly 88 years to the moment when the *Royal Edward* sank, I laid my flowers as I had intended. It was still and, apart from the sound of distant rush-hour traffic, quiet and calm. No one else was there: just me. I found myself bowing my head as a mark of respect, not only to those

Kettering War Memorial, Northamptonshire, England, Wednesday 13 August 2003, 0900hrs. *Author*

remembered from the *Royal Edward* but to all those whose lives had ended so prematurely so long ago. And yet, through my research on this project, they all seemed that much closer to me. The First World War may have been consigned to the history books, but to me it was a living, breathing entity. It had happened, and all of those youngsters, all those names on memorials everywhere, had died for their God, King and Country. That's just how it was in those days. They had died for the preservation of the future. It just seemed to me that we *still* owe them so much. We must *still* remember and give thanks.

That day I still had a programme to present for the BBC, which meant that my presence would be required post-haste at the studios in Northampton. Naturally I had mentioned the events that morning to both my Producer and the Assistant Editor, and both agreed that some mention should be made in my programme that lunchtime.

For the previous two and a half years I had been presenting a lunchtime current affairs/consumer and phone-in programme that was broadcast live each weekday between 12 noon and 2 o'clock. During the first hour of the show that day I decided to give a much edited narration of what had happened to the *Royal Edward* 88 years ago. The response from listeners was breathtaking – most emotional. People were calling me with tales of the men from the region who had died. Some just called in wanting more information – names, photographs, dates. It was an odd experience in many ways because here were the voices of the people who knew the lads from the ship – the same folk who keep pictures of those forever-young men on their mantles, because here for the first time the story of their loved ones was being told. Moreover, their story was being broadcast via the BBC on the anniversary date of the tragedy. Again it was brought home to me that people would never forget their boys.

Following the broadcast that day the Assistant Editor, Laura Moss, sent me an unexpected congratulatory e-mail that I shall treasure as part of this entire project.

'I'm sorry I didn't get a chance to speak to you after today's programme but I just wanted to say how powerful I thought the HMT *Royal Edward* piece was. The way you told the story Richard made for a compelling listen and it was great to hear the callers responding as well…'

These days millions of tourists visit the beautiful islands of Greece, the spectacle that is Santorini and the playgrounds of Crete. It's strange to me to think that anyone or any nation would use such a balmy location as a killing ground. Yet many thousands of lives were lost, on all sides, during the Great War and in the vastness of the blue-green Aegean.

I was determined to get as close to the *Royal Edward* as possible to see if I might feel something, anything. I therefore set about the planning of a trip to the last known co-ordinates of the ship. I guess it also seemed the ideal way to end this story – the best conclusion I could think of.

I needed to find the nearest inhabited Greek island that could be used as a base from which to launch some kind of an expedition. I figured that the only way to reach my objective was to fly directly to the island of Kos and to transfer to the much smaller and lesser-known Nisyros. That would be the ideal spot.

By July 2003 the wheels of travel were put into motion, complete with a somewhat sketchy initial itinerary drawn up. This would see us spending a week in Mandraki on Nisyros island – perfect. The thought of visiting the actual site of the sinking filled me with a mixture of emotions, not least of which were excitement, sadness and humility. After all, this is a vast war grave.

A one-off visit of this nature would have to be marked in some way. I therefore decided to explore the idea of dropping some kind of engraved stone into the sea as a permanent memorial. I had set my

My granite memorial plaque. *Author*

In silent memory of those who lost their lives
Here or near this place

36° 31' N - 26° 51' E

H.M.T ROYAL EDWARD

Destroyed at a time of world conflict
Friday 13ᵃ August 1915

RO NN173DE ENGLAND 7.9.2003

heart on a double-sided engraved piece of granite that would ideally rest as close as possible to the *Royal Edward*. However, there was the cost to consider. One quote for the job was in the region of £650, which was completely prohibitive given our tight budget. Eventually, and after re-evaluating the number of letters to be included on the memorial stone, I managed to get a quote of £150.00 – quite a difference, I'm sure you'll agree!

The route would be south-west from Nisyros island, past Kandhelioussa island with its small 19th-century lighthouse, then directly west for another 6 miles or so until we reached the exact co-ordinates: latitude 36° 31' North, longitude 26° 51' East. Of course, a great deal depended upon the availability and cost of an ocean-going vessel that might carry us to the exact location. Some kind of satellite navigation system would be essential. I'd spoken with the Greeks by telephone and everything just seemed a little uncertain.

On the Friday before we left I recorded an interview with the BBC that would be 'played out' while we were in Greece – a kind of pre-emptive progress report. I had also arranged talks with a publisher that would take place on our return. Finally, the story will have been told of a grand old ship and those who had faced that final dawn with her. Sadly she wasn't the only one, but she was the first.

We arrived on Kos island from Gatwick on Wednesday 3 September 2003. After only a short taxi ride of some 10 minutes or so we arrived at the holiday resort of Kardamena. We'd explained to the driver that we needed to make some kind of a ferry or boat connection to the island of Nisyros, and as he dropped us off he indicated that we needed to find our way down to the harbour via a short pedestrian area of about a hundred yards. A woman in a small tourist office confirmed that the boat we saw nodding in the distance would be heading for Nisyros within the next 2 hours.

Standing on the quay was the first chance we'd had to really catch our breath that day, to relax. Sure, there was a definitive purpose to this trip, but there was no reason not to enjoy the fabulous Greek sunshine. I donned my rolled-up Panama and sunglasses to take a look at the small seaside town in which we found ourselves. Sadly, if one removed the bars and restaurants there would be precious little left. Yet God knows, that's just what it needed. The British were certainly leaving their mark, that much was obvious. We both agreed that this was a place not to be deliberately re-visited.

I had been speaking to the ship's engineer, a heavy-set chap called Nick, who spoke very good American English. He told us of his ten years working in New York. Naturally I began to fish for ideas as to how I might travel from Nisyros to the exact co-ordinates of the *Royal Edward*. Indeed, we didn't even know what Nisyros looked like or how many people lived there. We only knew that it was the nearest inhabited island to where the *Royal Edward* lay. It seemed to me that the boat we were sitting on would be ideal for the purpose: she was about 70 feet long with a wide beam, and could certainly handle the open sea. The cost of such a trip would be another major factor, I knew that. But I also knew that Nick, a very affable and talkative type, might mention the affair to his captain.

Just a few locals boarded for the one-hour crossing together with a few crates of tomatoes and vegetables. Caroline and I spent the entire trip on the top deck enjoying the sunshine. There was not another soul up top, which made the experience quite special. However, after about 10 minutes into the journey, the captain came up the stairs to collect our 12-euro fare. He was a small man of about 60 with skin like old leather. As he collected the money he simply looked directly at me, mentioned his conversation with Nick and, before any discussion or negotiation could take place, threw out a figure of 700 euros for the job. He then made it clear that this was non-negotiable, his justification being the sheer running cost of a boat that size, the time and the hiring of a two or three man crew for a return seaward journey. I looked at him straight and told him no. I then tried to reason or negotiate, but he was having none of it. Before another word could be spoken he was gone, leaving me to lick my wounds on the upper deck of his boat.

I was deeply despondent. Yet Caroline remained optimistic, saying that other opportunities would present themselves. I really hoped she was right. After all, the engraved piece of granite in my shoulder bag was growing heavier by the minute and I had been so determined all along that it should rest on the sea bed as close to the *Royal Edward* as possible. I had even had the bloody thing dated!

The owner of our hotel, which had been booked well in advance, met our boat at Mandraki harbour. What did surprise us both was the closeness of the hotel to the harbour – all of 300 yards – yet here was this man to collect us with his van. I found this impressive.

Nisyros is a very small volcanic island, and its only real visitors come in the shape of red-skinned day-trippers from Kos, its much larger neighbour. Both islands are part of a larger group of Greek islands known as the Dodecanese, which lie just to the west of the Turkish coastline. The tourists arrive at 10 in the morning and are gone by 4 in the afternoon. It's rare that anyone other than Greeks spends a week on Nisyros. This alone made us a novelty on the island.

Our hotel, the Haritos, was the only hotel on the island with a swimming pool (salt water), which suited Caroline down to the ground. She loves water. I, on the other hand, don't. I have always had a fear of water – a genuine dread, a deep-seated phobia. Hence I can't swim, yet I truly admire those that can. So, while Caroline embedded herself in a poolside lounger I decided to explore a little bit of our 'base' village of Mandraki, accompanied by my notebook and my *Royal Edward* slab of granite.

Near the quayside was a small, white, stand-alone, well-maintained building that, I had later found out, used to be a public lavatory. Outside was a sign that read 'Enetikon Travel'. This was Thursday morning and I needed to find a captain and a boat for a sea trip that coming Sunday, as that was the date on the piece of granite. A travel company like this might know someone that would fit the bill.

Behind the desk sat a young lady who, thankfully, understood English and who seemed almost immediately to grasp the urgency of my request. I showed her my book in rough form and, of course, the ever-present engraved granite. She told me to come back in about 30 minutes as the proprietor was currently tied up at the harbour with tourists. She told me not to worry and that she would be sure to explain everything to her boss.

Sure enough, 30 minutes later I returned to the little white building. This time I was greeted by a very bubbly character called Michelle. Michelle had married a Greek man and had lived on Nisyros for a number of years. Her Greek, although I'm not the best judge, seemed perfect, and in Michelle I was to find a real gem of a contact. Michelle ran the place while her husband Nikos ferried tourists back and forth from Kos. Next to Michelle sat Mike, a bearded Englishman formerly of Islington. He and his partner Suzanne really had escaped: they had sold up everything and had arrived with just a few cases on Nisyros five years earlier to start a new life of 'quality'.

Michelle, after hearing first hand my story of the *Royal Edward* and how I desperately needed a boat for Sunday, immediately started making phone calls. She asked me to sit and wait while she made her enquiries. Eventually, after about 20 minutes, she said she had found a boat-owner who would be willing to negotiate on price and the finer details. He would meet me at Michelle's office that same evening at 8 o'clock. I was ecstatic. I thanked Michelle and Mike for looking after me and headed back to Caroline at her poolside.

At that stage all I knew of the *Royal Edward*'s final resting-place was that it was approximately 6 miles west of the remote lighthouse islet of Kandhelioussa. No one that I had spoken to on Nisyros had ever heard of the *Royal Edward*, let alone the fact that a piece of 20th-century history had taken place on their doorstep. Even their local parliamentary representative was intrigued – that someone like me should be introducing them to the facts. One man even suggested that the plaque should be seen by all, and would be better placed on the wall of the Town Hall or perhaps the Town Square.

That evening, Caroline and I made our way to Michelle's office for a meeting with a captain. We all shook hands and, following the usual pleasantries, got down to business. He had been briefed on the co-ordinates as he sat behind a huge desk studying a nautical map of the Aegean. He confirmed that if the price were right he would do the job. Indeed, he'd even brought his crew with him.

Following my previous day's experience with a certain other captain, I was a little wary. Yet this chap seemed very sincere and simply asked us to name a price. Well, after a deal of toing and froing the remarkably low figure of 200 euros was agreed. Even I knew that this was a bargain given all the factors involved.

Out of curiosity I asked to see his charts. He turned the huge piece of paper round so I might get a better view. There in front of me was the exact location of the *Royal Edward*. The circled 'X' marked the spot.

It was a very emotional moment for me. It also unclouded my mind. It was clear that the task at hand was a big one, involving a trip of some 3 or 4 hours in deep open sea. It would appear that the *Royal Edward* sank at a depth of around 502 metres (approximately 1,646 feet). I began to panic slightly, but I would not be deterred. It was also noticeable that original reports of the sinking had been quite basic. She was lying more like 8 miles north-west of Kandhelioussa and south-west from Nisyros. We all smiled, shook hands and said goodnight. The agreement was to meet at the harbour on Sunday morning at 1030hrs. Still very anxious, I was nevertheless incredibly excited.

Later that evening I tried to imagine the breathtaking depth at which the *Royal Edward* lay. How far would my plaque have to travel before resting on the seabed or wherever? I began to think in terms of the world's tallest buildings to give it all some perspective. The Petronas Towers in Kuala Lumpur stand 1,483 feet high – still some 160 feet short of the depth of the *Royal Edward*! The former US World Trade Center Twin Towers stood at a mere 1,368 feet tall.

There was one very important factor that

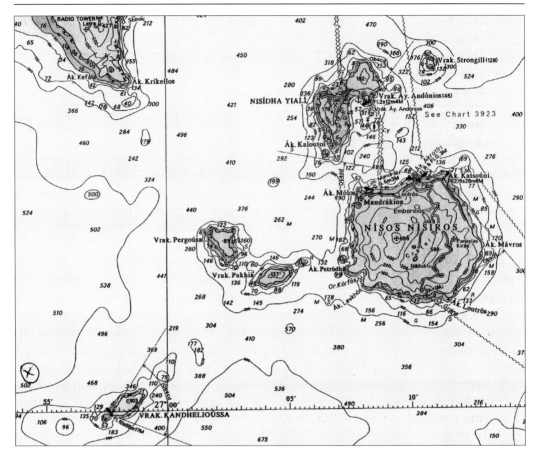

'X' marks the spot (bottom left)! *Author's collection*

everyone seemed to have overlooked, and, dare I say, had taken very much for granted. The weather. Up to this point the weather had been glorious and typical for this region at this time of the year: hot and still. This was certainly the case on the Wednesday and the Thursday. However, the next day was to change everything. As we looked out to sea on the Friday morning from our window at the Haritos, we just couldn't believe our eyes. Huge waves whipped up by gale-force winds were battering the coastline directly in front of the hotel. Long grasses next to the hotel, that looked like Japanese knotweed, were being forced flat by the power of the wind coming directly at us from the sea. There would be no tourist boats today. There

would be no boats leaving the island either, which would be tough should one have a flight to catch from Kos. Without exaggeration it was a wind that could lift you off your feet and cause serious damage to property. At any other time, given any other circumstance, I might have seen the beauty in this aspect of a powerful element – however, my sights were firmly fixed on Sunday's expedition and none of this was helping.

All was still looking grim as we looked out on the Saturday. If anything, the weather had become worse, yet the locals seemed quite adamant that conditions would improve. All we could do was hope that they would be right – I just couldn't see it myself. I kept looking at the inscribed lump of granite laying on my bed and wishing that I hadn't had the thing dated. How conceited was that! We held our breath.

Sunday arrived and I remember feeling somewhat optimistic. The winds had died, the sea appeared to be calmer and the tall grasses were no longer flat. Perhaps we would be lucky. We packed all our things together for the sea journey and headed down to the harbour. There was a definite breeze, but surely that couldn't make much of a difference, could it? Anyway, we were the first to arrive, so took the opportunity to take a few photographs of the plaque as a permanent record of the day. The time was approaching 1015hrs so we began to walk up to Michelle's office to find out what was happening. A solemn-faced Mike met us.

'Bad news, I'm afraid. The trip's off today – it's still too windy for the boat to face the open sea. I'm sorry.'

I began to think that the trip was just never going to happen. Caroline suggested that we go back down to the harbour for a coffee and wait for the captain to come in, just to get the story from his lips.

Eventually we were all down at the harbour as the tourist boats began to arrive again, following the high winds of the last couple of days. Michelle and Mike were busy allocating and collecting tickets and I sat at a table with Suzanne and Caroline. Eventually our illustrious captain's boat appeared, chugging into the harbour and loaded with red-faced visitors. They all disembarked right in front of us and eventually the captain saw us. He came right over to me and apologised most profusely, shaking his head, shrugging his shoulders – you know the kind of thing. Let's face it, it wasn't his fault. The weather can't be forced to change. Sadly, he was unable to work for us on the Monday as he had his tourist trade to think about. Anyway, there sat the granite plaque on the table and passers-by were naturally curious and were stopping to read the inscription or to ask questions. Unknown to me some of these folk were other local seafarers who'd heard that a captain had turned down a job because of the weather. I also heard later that there was a great deal of discussion going on behind the scenes as to the value that should be placed on such a journey and the size of vessel capable of carrying out such a task.

Then, from out of nowhere, a young guy ran over to our table and told me that his captain would be willing to take us. I was just carried along by the whole thing and got rather excited as the teenager led me on to this rather large tourist cruiser. Inside, towards the front, was a slim, good-looking Greek guy. It was obvious from our first meeting that here was a man who knew what he wanted. We shook hands. He wasn't interested in small talk – he already knew who we were and why we were there.

'400 euros. I'll do it for 400 euros.'

I swallowed hard as I remembered my last failed attempt to barter with a captain on his own boat. 'No negotiation?' I asked rather timidly. He just smiled and said nothing. I decided I would just check on our finances with Caroline. She simply said that we had come all this way to get the job done, and we could find the money from somewhere. I went back on board to tell him yes. We shook hands and agreed that tomorrow at around the same time would be good.

This captain turned out to be Michelle's husband, which everyone, including Caroline, seemed to know. Everyone, that is, except me.

On Monday 8 September 2003 it was all systems go. We'd been told that the open sea might be a little rough, but at least today we would get to finish the job – to pay our respects. As we boarded the cruiser *Agios Konstantinos* it was clear that her captain, Nikolaos Stavrianos, was ready for the off. He'd assembled a mechanic and a trusty deck hand, George Tsoukalas and Nikos Kalidoni respectively, and I was beginning to feel very excited. People were taking photographs right, left and centre. I held my plaque proudly between my hands, not really knowing if I should smile or not. After all, this was a relatively solemn occasion. Yet I reminded myself that this was also a day to celebrate the lives of those young men and to mark

The *Agios Konstantinos.* *Author*

The author (left) with Captain Nikolaos Stavrianos. *Author*

their graves for ever. Also joining us that day was Michelle's father, Bill McKann, Suzanne and the captain's son Kostas Stavrianos. Caroline would be in charge of the video and all photography. Some beer was placed aboard as refreshment for the crew.

At about 11.15hrs the boat slowly moved away from the quayside as we waved to Mike, Michelle and her mother Marlene. Once we had cleared the small harbour of Mandraki the captain, Nikos, opened the throttle and we were off, heading west. He'd plotted the course carefully and with the help of the on-board satellite navigation system estimated a running time of around 90 minutes or so to reach the last co-ordinates of the *Royal Edward.*

At first the trip felt like any other tourist excursion, passing the whole town of Mandraki on our portside with its tiny monastery perched precariously high above the sea. It was a hot, beautiful day. Caroline was already using her video and taking photographs of our surroundings. I rested on the railing of the lower deck just chatting away to Suzanne. I had been told that there is sea, and there is *sea*. This meant that we should expect things to get significantly rougher as we headed away from the protection of the Greek islands and on into open sea with nothing in front of us except horizon. I went up on to the top deck with Caroline and thought how strange this vessel looked with only us as passengers – well, eight of us. The boat would normally be full of tourists being ferried between Kos and Nisyros.

Suddenly Caroline got very excited. Through her video lens close-up she had spotted an island to our left that had all the hallmarks of Kandhelioussa. God knows she had heard me talk about it so many times. We checked the charts below and sure enough, through a kind of distant haze, we were adjacent to the old 19th-century lighthouse. My mind was on the job, but my stomach was beginning to hate me. We had certainly hit rougher water and I was beginning to feel very seasick. I

tried so hard to concentrate, but my stomach was having none of it. I can't remember the last time I was ill while travelling, and this has to be the worst kind of travel sickness.

We had passed the last sight of Kos on our starboard side as we maintained a course ever westward. I just couldn't believe how rough the sea was and began to wonder if all of this was worth the trouble. I then had to mentally slap myself out of such a negative train. Of course it was bloody worth it. What's a bit of seasickness when there's a job to be done!

I spoke to no one as the bow continued to thunder down into the surf – left, right, up, down. I just kept myself to myself as my sickness became worse and worse.

Suddenly, or at least it seemed rather sudden, the boat's engines were cut. We began to turn around. Caroline was already with the captain and was there to witness the sat-nav LED indicate the exact last known co-ordinates of the *Royal Edward.*

We were now, according to all records, sitting right on top of her.

There had only been two other known deliberate visits to this location for the purposes of memorial for those that had died. The first time was when the *Devanha* sailed from Alexandria and arrived at the spot on the evening of Saturday 14 August 1915, as described above. The 14th is also significant for the people of Nisyros, as it heralds the start of the feast of 'Panagia Spiliani' or Virgin Mary, a public celebration that lasts two days. Then, some time during April 1934, the Canadian Pacific liner *Duchess of Richmond* was on her way to the war graves of Gallipoli when a lady and a padre offered prayers and laid a wreath upon the waves, again as described earlier On this day it was me standing on board a small boat that was tossing about on the deep waters of the Aegean. I had come a long way to get to this point. It had been almost a year since Uncle Alex in Vancouver had given me the faded photograph of Willie. It had taken that time to find his birthplace and now to stand over

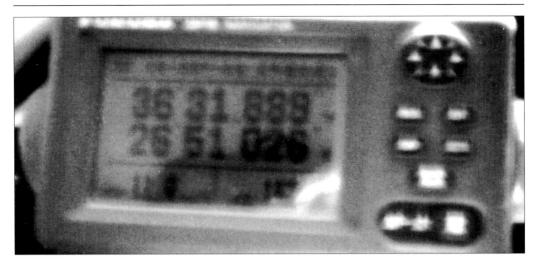

Latitude 36° 31' North, longitude 26° 51' East – we were on top of her! *Author*

his grave and the graves of so many. The thought made me feel so humble and the sea made me feel so vulnerable.

I hurriedly went inside the main cabin to collect the few bits that would be needed within the next few minutes. My head was spinning.

I had given great thought to what I might say at a moment like this before sending my beloved engraved tablet to the seabed. The captain, his crew, Suzanne, Bill, Caroline and myself were all now assembled on the lower deck starboard rear of the *Agios Konstantinos*. I turned to look at them, then picked up my clear aqua-coloured plastic envelope. Prior to our trip, Caroline had gathered a small bunch of Bougainvillaea flowers that had been growing naturally by the roadside just outside Mandraki. That little bunch now sat on the steps beside where I stood. Next to them, on the same step, a fine slab of British granite. Inside the envelope was a page of text that I had written two weeks in advance for this precise moment. Remember that I was still fighting off the terrible effects of seasickness.

'I just want to say a few words.' (Cough and slight pause.)

'There are no roses on sailors' graves,
Nor wreaths upon the storm tossed waves,
No last post…'

At this point I found myself struggling slightly and had to look to sea momentarily.

'…from the Royals band,
So far away from their native land,
No heartbroken words carved on stone,
Just shipmates' bodies there alone,
The only tributes are the seagulls' sweeps,
And the teardrop when a loved one weeps.'

'Well, here are the flowers.' At this point I picked up Caroline's small posy of Bougainvillaea and tossed it overboard. The petals reminded me so much of the poppy.

'…from those that care
And words on stone, the who, the where.'

'In special memory of
William Duncan Dick Nimmo
With love from your Mum & Dad
and all those who loved and missed you.

In memory of all that perished when

HMT *Royal Edward* was destroyed at this location
On Friday 13th August 1915.

For all the Canadian Mercantile Mariners
and their Captain.
For all from the Royal Army Medical Corps,
and all the young soldiers that died that day.

You are no longer lost at sea. Your grave is now
marked.'

I picked up the plaque from the ship's step.

'May you rest in peace for ever.'

I then put down the envelope containing these words and leaned over the side with the plaque in both hands. I kissed it then let it slip from my fingers. I was immediately surprised at the way my weighty piece of granite performed after it entered the water. It shot sideways left, then sideways right, almost taking a last look at us from the clear blue of the surface water. Then, and very quickly, it seemed to roll over and shoot impatiently into the deep under the boat. It was gone. I caught myself smiling as I wiped away a tear.

* * *

Finding an ending to a tale like this is almost as difficult as finding the beginning. So many lives were lost in both World Wars and the other conflicts that peppered the 20th century. The story of this ship is but one of hundreds of nautical nightmares that could, and should, be told. I have already closed my eyes and tried to imagine my granite plaque 'landing' on the seabed, after a long, dark downward journey. Did it stay in one piece? Did it land on its edge? Did it land close to, or even on, the *Royal Edward*? Well, the truth is that no one will ever know. She lies too deep.

People have said to me that life is for the living and we shouldn't dwell on the past. I agree. However, I also believe that there are some things that should always remain in the conscious mind of every decent, free person: the sacrifices that were made so that others might live in peace. Mind you, I should love to bring up the ship's bell. It ought to be displayed somewhere like Glasgow, Toronto, Bristol or even Nisyros. I wonder how one might go about organising a dangerous and expensive expedition like that? Now, there's a thought…!

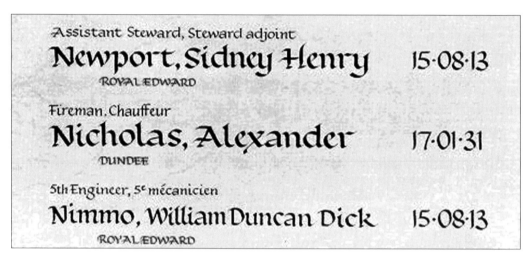

Assistant Steward, Steward adjoint
Newport, Sidney Henry   15·08·13
ROYAL EDWARD

Fireman, Chauffeur
Nicholas, Alexander   17·01·31
DUNDEE

5th Engineer, 5ᵉ mécanicien
Nimmo, William Duncan Dick   15·08·13
ROYAL EDWARD

William Nimmo's name in one of the Canadian Books of Remembrance, containing the names of Canadians who fought in wars and died either during or after them. All the books are kept in the Memorial Chamber located in the Peace Tower on Parliament Hill in Ottawa. *Author's collection*

HMT *Royal Edward* Roll of Honour

Some of the Canadian mercantile mariners who lost their lives
when the *Royal Edward* foundered on Friday 13 August 1915

Commander Peter Millman Wotton RNR
Master and Captain of the *Royal Edward*

Barnard Charles Spaul	Chief Officer
Hugh Tilsley	1st Mate
Charles Harold Boddey	Chief Engineer
Herbert Molyneux Stubbs	2nd Engineer
Ernest Arthur Mathew Bannister	2nd Engineer
Charles Maddock Parry	3rd Engineer
Herbert Rees	3rd Engineer
Alan Douglas Clapham	5th Engineer
William Duncan Dick Nimmo	5th Engineer
Alexander Hamilton	Boatswain
George Joseph Dunne	Boatswain's mate
William Jonathan Williams	Chef
Henry John Shergold	2nd Chef
James Thomas	Cook
Frederick Albert Victor Avery	Assistant Cook
Clarence Fogwell	Troop Cook
Harry William Downing	1st Pantryman
Francis Sewell Stebbing	2nd Pantryman
Tom Duckham	Sculleryman
Walter Henry Hobbs	Sculleryman
George Monks	Sculleryman
Percival Harold Stedeford	Sculleryman
Albert Arthur Burchett	Baker and confectioner

Ivor Bertie Jones	Assistant Baker
Albert James Loring	Assistant Butcher
Sydney Higgins Peters	Assistant Butcher
Arthur James Winter	2nd Storekeeper
Benjamin John Brooks	Assistant Storekeeper
Charles Watson	Supercargo
Tom Warland Cooper	Chief Steward
James Quayle	Master's Steward
George Albert Wines	Officers' Steward
Eric Thomas Jones	Engineers' Steward
Francesco William Barral	1st Cabin Steward
Alexander Symon	2nd Steward
Alfred Echevarri	1st Salon Steward
Alexander William Skimming	2nd Salon Steward
Leonard Duffner	Assistant Steward
A. Golding	Assistant Steward
George Henry Llewellyn	Assistant Steward
Sidney Henry Newport	Assistant Steward
Reginald Parsons	Assistant Steward
Thomas Moore Shillinglaw	Assistant Steward
Frederick William Simmons	Assistant Steward
Thomas McLeod	Troop Deck Steward
William Paterson Saunders	Canteen and Troop Deck Steward
Henry Brown	Carpenter

Joseph Howard Body	Writer
Spero Argyros	Able-bodied Seaman
Karl Frykman	Able-bodied Seaman
William Kinsella	Able-bodied Seaman
O. Benson	Able-bodied Seaman
August Lesburg	Able-bodied Seaman
Reginald Arthur Jubilee Pretlove	Ordinary Seaman
Alfred Williams	Ordinary Seaman
Patrich Devaney	Seaman
D. Hansen	Seaman
K. Johansson	Seaman
William Joseph Nolan	Seaman
Joseph Poirier	Seaman
T. Pentson	Seaman
Herbert Tom Sedlen	Seaman
A. Velasquez	Seaman
Thomas Ashton*	Trimmer
Henry Thomas Hart*	Trimmer
William George Burchill	Trimmer
J. Cusson	Trimmer
John Edward Francis	Trimmer
Thomas William Hodgkins	Trimmer
J. Hughes	Trimmer
Charles Albert Hunt	Trimmer
Henry William King	Trimmer
John Larkin	Trimmer
James Long	Trimmer
William Page	Trimmer
William Parsons	Trimmer
Christopher Power	Trimmer
John Edward Pullin	Trimmer
J. Ross	Trimmer
David Sweeney	Trimmer
Worthy Winkworth	Trimmer

*On the Tower Hill Memorial in London, it clearly states that Henry Thomas Hart served as Thomas Ashton.

Samuel Pollock	Refrigeration Greaser
Joseph George Bull	Greaser
William George Colston Genley	Greaser
William Jones	Greaser
Reginald Williams	Greaser

Those with unknown rank or title

J. N. Usher (served as J. N. Edwardes)	
J. W. Clines	
Fitzgerald	
J. J. Padden	
L. Pritchard	
M. Royton	
C. Sadler	
J. W. Stewart	
Pauli Adami	Fireman
William Anderson	Fireman
Pierre Apers	Fireman
Domenica Borg	Fireman
Percival Leonard E. Brooks	Fireman
J. Carney	Fireman
John Costello (served as J. Cushley)	Fireman
Stratis Costinas	Fireman
J. A. de Bruin	Fireman
Emannuelle Depares	Fireman
Paulo Ferrugia	Fireman
K. Druselius	Fireman
Guiseppe Galea	Fireman
Mike Gretch	Fireman
Frank Ewart Griffiths	Fireman
A. Hammar	Fireman
William Hart	Fireman
W. Hilton	Fireman
John Hoolahan	Fireman
K. Janson	Fireman
Albert Thomas Lemon	Fireman
N. Lusis	Fireman
Stanley Mack	Fireman
Gugliania Mallia	Fireman
James Meakin	Fireman
Giovanni Montebello	Fireman
Carruana Paul	Fireman

Zara Paulo	Fireman	John Scullion	Fireman
Joseph Pirata	Fireman	H. Thomas	Fireman
Luca Psaila	Fireman	D. Trapanese	Fireman
S. Romero	Fireman	Fideli Zammit	Fireman
James Scullion	Fireman		

The following is a comprehensive list of the British officers and servicemen that died.
They are listed within their own regiments and in alphabetical order. Some of the officers were on
attachment from other regiments.
b. born, e. enlisted, r. resided

The Royal Army Medical Corps (Territorial Force)

DAUBER, John Henry, Lt-Col
HAYHURST, Thomas, Lt
MARSHALL, Charles Bertram, Capt
MOWAT, James, Major

ALCOCK, Tom, e. Burnley, Lancs, 538, Private
ALLDRIDGE, William John, e. Chelmsford, Essex, 68, A/L/Cpl
ALTHAM, Arthur, e. Burnley, Lancs, 516, Private
AVIS, Arthur John, e. Ipswich, Suffolk, 92, Private
BANNISTER, John Frederick, b. Chorley, Lancs, e. Manchester, Lancs, 480, Private
BARNARD, Simeon, b. Cinderford, Glos, e. Burnley, Lancs, 400, Private
BASSNETT, Frank, e. Burnley, Lancs, 566, Private
BATES, William Henry, e. Kettering, Northants, 112, Private
BEBBINGTON, Albert Edward, b. Old Trafford, Lancs, e. Manchester, Lancs, 458, Private
BENNETT, Joseph, b. Govan, Lanarkshire, e. Glasgow, Lanarkshire, 1811, Private
BIRCH, William Charles, e. Conisboro, Yorks, 127, Private
BLOOMFIELD, Ernest Edward, e. Ipswich, Suffolk, 2357, Private
BONESS, William Redman, e. Chelmsford, Essex, 69, Private
BONNEY, Charles, e. Manchester, Lancs, r. Middleton, Lancs, 536, Private

BRAYFIELD, Sam, e. Ipswich, Suffolk, r. Raunds, Northants, 109, Private
BRELSFORD, Harry, e. Burnley, Lancs, 462, Private
BROWN, George William, e. Lowestoft, Suffolk, 79, Private
BYWATER, Robert, b. Clayton, Lancs, e. Manchester, Lancs, 533, Private
CANN, Alfred Edward, e. Gt Yarmouth, Norfolk, 94, S/Sgt
CARTER, John Edwin, b. Tonge, Lancs, e. Bolton, Lancs, 315, Cpl
CHAMBERLAIN, Edward, b. Lowestoft, Suffolk, e. Ipswich, Suffolk, 5, Sgt
CHAMBERLAIN, Herbert Victor, e. Walthamstow, r. Leyton, Essex, 2158, Cpl
CLARK, Edward Joseph, e. Ipswich, Suffolk, 98, Cpl
CLARK, William Greig, e. Aberdeen, r. Fraserburgh, Aberdeenshire, 2061, Private
CLARKE, Ewart William, e. Luton, Beds, 82, Private
CLARKE, William Albert, e. Wath-on-Dearne, r. Rotherham, Yorks, 122, Private
CLAY, Christopher, e. Lowestoft, Suffolk, 72, Private
CLAYDON, Edward Thomas, b. Earls Colne, Essex, e. Ipswich, Suffolk, 14, Private
COATES, Reginald Rowland, e. Lowestoft, Suffolk, 83, Private

CODLING, Walter Stephen, e. Norwich, Norfolk, 95, Private

CONWAY, Joseph Patrick, b. Burnley, Lancs, e. Burnley, Lancs, 374, Private

COOPER, Horace, e. Ipswich, Suffolk, 2346, Private

COTTERELL, Percy Eglin, e. Cambridge, Cambs, 76, Cpl

CRANE, Charles William, e. Burnley, Lancs, 521, Private

CROSS, William Russell, e. Glasgow, r. Coatbridge, Lanarks, 1791, Private

DAVIDSON, Thomas, e. Aberdeen, Aberdeenshire, 2049, Private

DAVIES, Dan Hindley, b. Bradford, Yorks, e. Manchester, Lancs, 430, Private

DAVISON, Horace, e. Manchester, Lancs, r. Retford, Notts, 593, Private

DENT, Henry, b. Burnley, Lancs, e. Burnley, 388, Private

EATON, George, b. Bury St. Edmunds, Suffolk, e. Ipswich, Suffolk, 28, Private

FARRAR, John, e. Burnley, Lancs, 540, Private

FISHER, William, b. Ancoats, Lancs, e. Manchester, Lancs, 437, Private

FRASER, James Scott, e. Aberdeen, Aberdeenshire, 1998, Private

GARBETT, Enoch, b. Wath-on-Dearne, Yorks, e. Rotherham, Yorks, 130, Private

GARDINER, Charles Lewis, e. Saffron Walden, Essex, 99, Private

GODLEY, Edwin, e. Ipswich, r. Wickham Market, Suffolk, 64, Cpl

GREEN, Charles, e. Aberdeen, Aberdeenshire, 2000, Private

GREEN, Walter John, b. Needham Market, Suffolk, e. Ipswich, Suffolk, r. Cobham, Surrey, 42, Sgt

GREIG, George, e. Aberdeen, Aberdeenshire, 2050, Private

HALL, Harry Hayward, e. Lowestoft, Suffolk, 70, Private

HASLOP, Arthur Charles, e. Cambridge, Cambs, r. Trumpington, Cambs, 73, Private

HATHERLY, Louis, e. Burnley, Lancs, 513, Private

HAWKES, William, b. Manchester, Lancs, e. Manchester, Lancs, 274, A/Cpl

HAY, William Douglas, b. Ardwick, Lancs, e. Manchester, Lancs, 444, Private

HAYES, John Dennis, b. Bramford, Suffolk, e. Ipswich, Suffolk, 44, A/L/Cpl

HELLIWELL, Henry Cartwright, e. Manchester, Lancs, 433, Cpl

HOWARD, Clement, e. St. Helens, Lancs, 1676, Private

HOWARD, John Charles Tyrell, e. Kettering, Northants, 115, Private

HOWARTH, Ernest, b. Burnley, Lancs, e. Burnley, Lancs, 365, A/Sgt

HUGHES, Ernest, e. Kettering, Northants, 117, Private

HUNTER, John, e. Wath-on-Dearne, Yorks, r. Rotherham, Yorks, 131, Private

HUNTER, John Galbraith, b. Lennoxtown, Stirlingshire, e. Glasgow, Lanarks, r. Lennoxtown, 1776, Private

JOHNSON, Albert, e. Burnley, Lancs, 498, Private

JOHNSTON, Joseph, b. Hutchinsontown, Lanarks, e. Glasgow, Lanarks, 1766, Private

KENDALL, Patrick, e. Burnley, Lancs, 464, Private

KILBURN, Nelson, e. Burnley, Lancs, 415, Private

KNOWLES, Alfred, b. Rawtenstall, Lancs, e. Bolton, Lancs, 397, Private

LAKE, John, e. Norwich, Norfolk, r. New Walsingham, Norfolk, 96, Private

LE GRICE, Harold Charles, e. Ipswich, Suffolk, r. King's Lynn, Norfolk, 2351, Private

LEEDS, Claude Henry John, e. Lowestoft, Suffolk, 85, Private

LUFKIN, Francis John, e. Chelmsford, Essex, r. Braintree, Essex, 2344, Private

MALLETT, Robert Samuel, e. Lowestoft, Suffolk, 106, Private

MANSBRIDGE, John Allen, e. Wath-on-Dearne, Yorks, r. Rotherham, Yorks, 132, Private

McIVER, Norman, b. Dalziel, Lanarks, e. Glasgow, Lanarks, 1839, Private

McLAUGHLIN, Thomas, e. Manchester, Lancs, 592, Private

McMURDO, Edward Longdon, b. Edgbaston, Warks, e. Ipswich, Suffolk, r. Bury St. Edmunds, Suffolk, 41, S/Sgt

McNEARNIE, James, b. Penighame, Wigtownshire, e. Glasgow, Lanarks, 1780, Private

MIDGELEY, Charles, e. Burnley, Lancs, 448, Private

MOORE, Arthur, e. Burnley, Lancs, 469, Private

MORRISON, James, e. Aberdeen, Aberdeenshire, 2006, Private

MOSLEY, Leonard, e. Burnley, Lancs, 413, Private

MUNRO, James, e. Burnley, Lancs, 571, Private

NEWELL, James, e. Burnley, Lancs, 414, Private

NUTTALL, Albert Edmund, e. Ipswich, Suffolk, 2289, Private

NUTTALL, John Joseph, b. Whalley Bridge, Derbys, e. Manchester, Lancs, 448, Private

OLDFIELD, Charles Robert, e. Lowestoft, Suffolk, 80, Private

PIKE, Samuel Augustus, e. Ipswich, Suffolk, r. Cambridge, Cambs, 2350, Private

POPPY, Harry Charles, e. Lowestoft, Suffolk, 89, Private

PRICE, Alfred George, b. Shoreditch, London, e. Walthamstow, Essex, r. Canonbury, London, 2053, Private

PYOTT, Thomas James, e. Wath-on-Dearne, Yorks, r. Rotherham, Yorks, 125, A/L/Cpl

RAWSTRON, Fred, e. Burnley, Lancs, 410, Private

REYNOLDS, Frank, e. Lowestoft, Suffolk, 84, Private

RICHMOND, Fred, e. Burnley, Lancs, 563, Private

RIDING, Sidney, e. Manchester, Lancs, r. Preston, Lancs, 583, Private

ROBERTS, Ernest William, e. Lowestoft, Suffolk, 71, Sgt

ROGERS, Alee, e. Cambridge, Cambs, 103, Private

ROWE, Frederick George, e. Ipswich, Suffolk, 105, Private

ROWLAND, Frank Dennis, e. Woodbridge, Suffolk, 87, Sgt

RULE, William Alfred, e. Cambridge, Cambs, 78, Private

SHARMAN, Frederick, e. Ipswich, Suffolk, 2342, Private

SHEPHERD, Arthur, e. Manchester, Lancs, r. Rochdale, Lancs, 578, Private

SHUTTLEWORTH, James Alan, e. Burnley, Lancs, 515, Private

SIMMIE, Robert Hill Leighton, b. Lochie, Forfarshire, e. Glasgow, Lanarks, 1794, Private

SIMMONS, George William, e. Ipswich, Suffolk, r. Felixstowe, Suffolk, 2329, Private

SIMMS, Frederick, b. Putney, Surrey, e. Manchester, Lancs, 443, Private

SIMPSON, Ernest, b. St. Marks, Lancs, e. Manchester, Lancs, 77, Private

SINCLAIR, James Anderson, b. Cowlairs, Lanarks, e. Glasgow, Lanarks, 1764, Private

SMITH, Henry William, e. Lowestoft, Suffolk, 75, Private

SMITH, John, e. Mexborough, Yorks, r. Conisborough, Yorks, 128, Private

SNELL, Robert Charles, e. Ipswich, Suffolk, 67, Sgt

STANBRIDGE, Charles, e. Aberdeen, Aberdeenshire, 2013, Sgt

STARKIE, Leonard, e. Burnley, Lancs, 555, Private

STARKIE, Walter, e. Burnley, Lancs, 547, Private

STEVENS, Frederick Arthur, e. Ipswich, Suffolk, 2343, Private

STEVENS, Thomas, e. Burnley, Lancs, 581, Private

STEVENSON, Charles, b. Milngavie, Lanarks, e. Glasgow, Lanarks, r. Edinburgh, 1803, L/Cpl

STEVENSON, William, e. Burnley, Lancs, r. Hopton, Staffs, 452, Private

STOCKDALE, Frank, b. Ordsall, Notts, e. Manchester, Lancs, 460, Private

STUBBS, Albert Victor, e. Ipswich, Suffolk, 136, Private

STUDD, Gaston Reginald, e. Ipswich, Suffolk, r. Bury St. Edmunds, Suffolk, 2340, Private

SUMMERFIELD, James, e. Kettering, Northants, 116, Private

THOMAS, William, e. Lowestoft, Suffolk, 91, Private

TOSELAND, Ernest Walter, e. Kettering, Northants, 114, Private

TURNER, Harry, e. Manchester, Lancs, 553, Private

UNDERWOOD, Ernest, b. Hulme, Lancs, e. Manchester, Lancs, 38, Cpl

VESEY, Walter Frank, e. Ipswich, Suffolk, 2345, Private

WALKER, Thomas, b. Chapel-en-le-Frith, Derbys, e. Manchester, Lancs, 450, Private

WATSON, Percy, e. Ipswich, Suffolk, r. Raunds, Northants, 110, Private

WHALLEY, Frank, e. Burnley, Lancs, r. Padiham, Lancs, 524, Private

WHITEHEAD, John Thomas, b. Burnley, Lancs, e. Burnley, 426, Private

WHITFALL, Alfred Charles, c. Burnley, Lancs, 497, Private

WHITTAKER, George Frederick Keswick, e. Burnley, Lancs, 468, Private

WHITTAKER, John Robert, e. Burnley, Lancs, 575, Private

WILD, Tom Harry, c. Wath-on-Dearne, Durham, 124, Cpl

WILKINSON, Fred, e. Burnley, Lancs, 529, Private

WILKINSON, Harrison, e. Burnley, Lancs, 496, Private

WILLS, Fred, e. Ipswich, Suffolk, r. Northampton, Northants, 135, Private

WILLS, Herbert, e. Kettering, Northants, 119, Private

WISEMAN, Harry, e. Burnley, Lancs, 487, Private

WOODS, James, b. St. Matthews, Suffolk, e. Ipswich, Suffolk, 137, Private

WORLEDGE, Charles, e. Ipswich, Suffolk, 133, Cpl

WORSWICK, Edgar, e. Burnley, Lancs, r. Padiham, Lancs, 465, Private

WRIGHT, William, b. Leith, Midlothian, e. Glasgow, Lanarks, 1765, Private

Corps of Royal Engineers

SHEPHERD, Robert John, b. Kilve, Somerset, e. London, r. Stoke Newington, Middx, 61704, Spr (11th Signal Coy, RE)

Cheshire Regiment – 1/4th Battalion

TUCKER, Timothy, e. Birkenhead, Cheshire, 2264, Private

Prince of Wales's Own (West Yorkshire Regiment) – 9th Battalion

WILSON, John William, b. Byker, Newcastle-on-Tyne, e. Newcastle-on-Tyne, 17483, Private

South Lancashire Regiment, Prince of Wales's Volunteers – 6th Battalion

GILL, John, b. St Helens, Lancs, e. St. Helens, 12374, Private

RIDGEWAY, William, b. Beswick, Lancs, e. Manchester, 12695, Private

The Royal Welsh Fusiliers – 8th Battalion

OTTLEY, William Richard, b. Marylebone, London, e. Rhyl, r. Meliden, Flint, 12468, Private

The Hampshire Regiment – 10th Battalion

HARDING, George, b. Southampton, Hants, e. Southampton, Hants, 10252, Private

The Manchester Regiment

ASHCROFT, John, e. Wigan, Lancs, 3181, Private, 1/5th Battalion

SHATWELL, Benjamin, b. Ashton-under-Lyne, Lancs, e. Audenshaw, Manchester, 2718, Private, 1/9th Battalion

The Welsh Regiment

CUTLER, Christopher, b. Wimbourne, Dorset, e. Cardiff, r. Tredegar, Mon, 11649, Private, 8th Battalion

DAVIES, John Elwyn, b. Carmarthen, e. Carmarthen, 4299, Private, 1/4th Battalion

JOHN, John, b. Llansamlet, Glam, e. Swansea, r. Landore, Glam, 27246, Sgt, 8th Battalion

LANGFORD, John, b. Neath, e. Neath, 12957, Private, 8th Battalion

The Royal Army Service Corps

BURTT, Edward, Lt (TP), (att'd 18/Lab Co), Royal Army Service Corps

LUND, William Bullen, Lt (TP), Royal Army Service Corps

ABREY, Thomas, b. St Pancras, Middx, e. London, r. Bow, London, SS/14124, Private

ASHDOWN, James Richard, b. Speldhurst, Kent, e. London, r. Tooting, Surrey, SS/13990, Private

BAKER, John Edwin, b. Brixton, Surrey, e. London, r. Stockwell, SS/14142, Private

BAKER, William, b. Lanteglos-by-Camelford, Cornwall, e. London, r. Falmouth, SS/14038, Private

BAMBERGER, Alexander, b. Walworth, Surrey, e. London, r. Westbourne Park, SS/13577, Private

BATTY, James, b. Cork, e. London, SS/13583, Private

BENNETT, Thomas George Cooper, b. Deptford, e. London, r. Falmouth, SS/14175, Private

BIDGOOD, Levi, b. Liskeard, Cornwall, e. London, r. Liskeard, SS/14112, Private

BIRD, John William, b. Islington, e. London, r. Dalston, SS/13838, Private

BOND, Thomas, b. St Blazey, Cornwall, e. London, r. Tywardreath Highway, SS/13894, Private

BONE, Harry, b. Falmouth, e. London, r. Falmouth, SS/14044, Private

BRAY, William, b. Truro, e. London, r. Truro, SS/13963, Private

BRYAN, Francis Henry, b. St Pancras, e. London, r. Lambeth, SS/13963, Private

BUDDLE, Edward James, b. Tuckingmill, Cornwall, e. London, r. Camborne, Cornwall, SS/14125, Private

CAHILL, Daniel, b. East Grinstead, e. London, r. Wandsworth, SS/13530, Private

CARPENTER, Richard, b. Bristol, e. London, r. St Blazey, Cornwall, SS/13909, Private

CAVILL, William James, b. Penrhyn, e. London, r. Falmouth, SS/14177, Private

CHITTY, William George, b. Rotherhithe, e. London, r. Tooting, SS/13982, Private

CLARKE, Alexander Herbert, b. Ealing, e. London, r. Wandsworth, SS/14002, Private

COLEMAN, Edward Bernard, b. Chichester, e. London, r. Marylebone, SS/13976, Private

COLLER, Frederick, b. Chelsea, e. London, r. Biscovey, Cornwall, SS/13893, Private

COLLOM, Edwin Albert, b. Camberwell, e. London, r. Southward, SS/13835, Private

COOK, John Walford, b. Fingringhoe, Essex, e. London, r. Mistley, SS13837, Private

CULPECK, William, b. Marylebone, e. London, r. Paddington, SS/13550, Private

DAVIES, Harry, b. Camberwell, e. London, r. Southwark, SS/13545, Private

DOBSON, Alfred, b. Runcorn, e. London, r. Falmouth, SS/14077, Private

DOLLMAN, Leonard Joseph, b. Brixton, e. London, r. King's Cross, SS/14153, Private

EATON, Edward Thomas, b. South Kensington, e. London, r. Kingston-on-Thames, SS/13533, Private

EDEN, Alfred, b. Deal, e. London, r. Pentewan, SS/13926, Private

EDWARDS, Benjamin Thomas, b. Southwark, e. London, r. West Norwood, SS/14118, Private

EMERY, Harold Richard, b. New Barnet, e. London, r. New Barnet, SS/14013, A/Cpl

ESLICK, William, b. Camborne, Cornwall, e. London, r. Redruth, SS/14123, Private

FINCH, Henry, b. Revelstoke, Devon, e. London, r. Newlyn East, Cornwall, SS/14260, Private

FITTOCK, Henry Harold, b. Falmouth, e. London, r. Falmouth, SS/14180, Private

FLOWERDAY, Charles, b. Lynn, Norfolk, e. London, r. Old Kent Road, SS/13998, Private

FRANKS, Henry, b. St Pancras, e. London, r. Pentonville, SS/13595, Private

FRIGGENS, Richard, b. Penzance, e. London, r. Penzance, SS/13538, Private

FRUIN, Joseph Thomas, b. Baldon, e. London, r. Wembley Hill, Middlesex, SS/14006, Private

GREEN, Thomas, b. St Blazey, e. London, r. Par, Cornwall, SS/13847, Private

GREEN, Wright, b. Leigh, Lancs, e. London, r. Tooting, SS/13975, Private

GREET, Caleb, b. Lanner, Cornwall, e. London, r. Grampound Road, Cornwall, SS/13944, Private

GRIFFITHS, John Davis, b. St Pancras, e. London, r. East Barnet, SS/14020, Private

GRIGG, Ernest, e. London, r. St Austell, SS/13921, Private

GURNEY, William, b. Kingston, e. London, r. Kilburn, SS/13135, Private

HARE, William Henry, b. Truro, e. London, r. Falmouth, SS/13851, Private

HARRIS, John, b. Kingston-on-Thames, e. London, r. Kingston-on-Thames, SS/13523, Private

HARVEY, Gilbert, b. Bermondsey, e. London, r. Bermondsey, SS/13794, Private

HEELEN, John, b. St Luke's, London, e. London, r. London EC, SS/13999, Private

HODGES, Alfred, b. Lambeth, e. London, r. St John's Wood, SS/13549, Private

HOSKIN, William James, b. St Austell, e. London, r. St Austell, SS/14107, Private

HOSKING, Frederick, b. Penzance, e. London, r. Penzance, SS/13539, Private

HOSKINS, James, b. Portsmouth, e. London, r. Penrhyn, SS/14182, Private

JAMES, Richard Joseph, b. Helston, Cornwall, e. London, r. Helston, SS/13844, Private

JONES, William Alliston, b. Fleet Street, City of London, e. London, r. Walworth, SS/14132, Private

JULEFF, William John, b. Ladock, Cornwall, e. London, r. St Austell, SS/13951, Private

KENT, Bridges Charles, b. St Issey, Cornwall, e. London, r. St Dennis, Cornwall, SS/13908, Private

KEVETH, Samuel, b. Launceston, Cornwall, e. London, r. St Austell, SS/13952, Private

KING, Francis Edward, b. Bedhampton, Hants, e. London, r. Kingston-on-Thames, SS/13670, Cpl

LAWS, William, b. Otford, Kent, e. London, r. Otford, SS/14010, Private

LOCKWOOD, John George, b. Bermondsey, e. London, r. Wandsworth, SS/2646, Private

LOVELL, Walter, b. Bath, e. London, r. Hove, SS/13542, Private

LOWE, William, e. London, r. Truro, SS/13941, Private

MANSFIELD, Robert Walker, b. Mile End, London, e. London, r. Mile End, SS/14009, Private

MARTIN, James, b. Trewen, Cornwall, e. London, r. St Austell, SS/14111, Private

MARTIN, Samuel, b. Tywardreath, Cornwall, e. London, r. St Austell, SS/13953, Private

MCCOOEY, Harry, b. Redruth, e. London, r. Devonport, SS/13906, Private

MEDLIN, Richard Thomas, b. Truro, Cornwall, e. London, r. Truro, SS/13956, Private

MICHELL, Ernest William, b. St Austell, e. London, r. Highgate, SS/13932, Private

MOORE, Albert, b. Bungay, Suffolk, e. London, r. Holborn, SS14115, Private

MOORE, Alfred, b. Falmouth, Cornwall, e. London, r. Falmouth, SS14056, Private

MOORE, George, b. Downham Market, Norfolk, e. London, r. Maidenhead, SS13872, Sgt

MORGAN, Mark, b. Willenhall, Staffs, e. London, r. Willenhall, SS/14003, Private

NETHERTON, Richard, b. Fowey, Cornwall, e. London, r. Par, Cornwall, SS/14179, Private

NORMAN, Charles Henry, b. Chester, e. London, r. Penzance, SS/13846, Private

O'NEIL, Thomas Alfred, b. Marylebone, e. London, r. Marylebone, SS/14152, Private

OLIVER, Thomas William, b. Watford, e. London, r. Watford, SS/13590, Private

OLNEY, Arthur, b. Westminster, e. London, r. Lambeth, SS/14000, Private

OPIE, William James, b. Perranwell, Cornwall, e. London, r. Penryn, SS/14089, Private

ORAM, Ernest Charles, b. Peterborough, e. London, r. Camberwell, SS/13372, Private

ORFORD, Albert George, b. Peckham, e. London, r. Peckham, SS/13988, Private

OSBORNE, Richard John, b. St Stephen's, Cornwall, e. London, r. Grampound Road, Cornwall, SS/13919, Private

PARKER, John Henry, b. Bethnal Green, e. London, r. Kensington, SS/14121, Private

PARRY, Richard George Nicholls, b. Wrexham, e. London, r. Walthamstow, SS/14122, Private

PASCOE, Hubert, b. Truro, e. London, r. Truro, SS/13948, Private

PEARCE, Frank, b. Gt Missenden, e. London, r. Wealdstone, SS/13589, Private

FELLOW, Richard Samuel, b. Penryn, Cornwall, e. London, r. Penryn, SS/14183, Private

PENROSE, Frederick, b. Truro, e. London, r. St Austell, SS/13916, Private

PETITT, George, b. New Barnet, Herts, e. London, r. New Barnet, SS/14019, Private

PETO, Albert Henry, e. London, r. Gt Missenden, Bucks, SS/13253, Private

PHILLIPS, James, b. Larkhall, Lanark, e. London, r. St Austell, Cornwall, SS/13955, Private

PHILLIPS, William, b. St Winnow, Cornwall, e. London, r. Truro, SS/13934, Private

POINTER, Frederick James, b. Westgate, e. Margate, r. Margate, SS/13242, Private

POLGLASE, Richard Henry, b. Helston, Cornwall, e. London, r. Helston, SS/13843, Private

PONSFORD, John, b. Truro, e. London, r. Truro, SS/13912, Private

PRATT, Edward Absalom, b. Hornsey, Middx, e. London, r. Hanwell, SS/13850, Private

RACHER, Walter, b. Wendy, Cambs, e. London, r. Earlsfield, SS/14059, Private

RICHARDS, Howard, b. Treverbyn, Cornwall, e. London, r. St Austell, SS/13931, Private

ROBERTS, Albert, b. Kentish Town, e. London, r. Highgate, SS/13552, Private

ROBERTS, Henry William, b. Clerkenwell, e. London, r. Islington, SS/13218, Private

ROBINS, William Henry, b. Kingstown, Co Cork, e. London, r. Mevagissey, Cornwall, SS/13876, Private

SANDON, Ernest Alfred, b. Clerkenwell, e. London, r. Clerkenwell, SS/13578, Private

SAYERS, James, b. Kentish Town, e. London, r. Islington, Middx, SS/12185, Private

SCOTT, Arthur Henry, b. Whitechapel, e. London, r. Old Ford, SS/14130, Private

SHEARER, James, b. Orkney, e. London, r. Westcliff-on-Sea, SS/12112, Private

SIMMONS, Harry, b. Truro, e. London, r. Truro, SS/13880, Private

SMITH, Alfred Ernest, b. Epsom, Surrey, e. London, r. Helston, Cornwall, SS/13903, Private

SMITH, John, b. Falmouth, e. London, r. Falmouth, SS/14037, Private

SPILLER, Frank William, b. Mabe, Cornwall, e. London, r. Penryn, Cornwall, SS/14110, Private

TAMBLYN, George Henry, b. Lostwithiel, Cornwall, e. London, r. Truro, SS/13938, Private

THOMAS, Joseph Waycott, b. Truro, e. London, r. Truro, SS/13940, Private

THOMSON, James, b. Edinburgh, e. London, r. Watford, SS/13840, Private

TRIPCONEY, Arthur, b. Falmouth, e. London, r. Falmouth, SS/14185, Private

TRURAN, William John, b. St Agnes, Cornwall, e. London, r. Redruth, SS/14087, Private

TUCKER, James Barry, b. St Columb, Cornwall, e. London, r. St Columb, SS/13853, Private

WALLER, Henry, b. Mereworth, Kent, e. London, r. Walworth, SS/14083, Private

WARNER, George, b. Spitalfields, Middx, e. London, r. Bethnal Green, SS/14060, Private

WATSON, Alfred, b. Greenwich, e. London, r. Falmouth, SS/14174, Private

WOODCHERRY, Joseph, b. Westminster, e. London, r. Lambeth, SS/14008, Private

WOON, Thomas Henry, b. Falmouth, e. London, r. Falmouth, SS/14204, Private

The Hampshire Regiment – 2nd Battalion

SPURWAY, Richard Popham, 2/Lt (TP), (att'd Hampshire Reg), Prince Albert's (Somerset Light Infantry), 2nd Battalion

THOMPSON, Edward Homer Boxwell, Lt (TP), (att'd Hampshire Reg), Prince Albert's (Somerset Light Infantry), 9th Battalion.

WEEKS, John, Temp 2/Lt, (att'd Hampshire Reg), Devonshire Regiment

ADAMS, William, b. Aston, Birmingham, e. Birmingham, 11741, Private

ALEXANDER, Henry James, b. Battersea, London, e. Holborn, London, r. Merton, Surrey, 11739, Private (formerly 13390, Duke of Cornwall's Light Infantry)

ALLEN, Norman Cecil, b. Sutton Scotney, Hants, e. Winchester, Hants, r. Sutton Scotney, Hants, 10474, Private

ASH, William Edward, b. Marylebone, London, e. Marylebone, London, r. Kilburn, London, 3/4377, Sgt

AXWORTHY, Edwin, b. Okehampton, Devon, e. Liskeard, Cornwall, 11738, Private(formerly 13369, Duke of Cornwall's Light Infantry)

BAKER, Frank, b. Rogate, Sussex, e. Aldershot, Hants, r. Rake, Hants, 10587, Private

BARNSLEY, Herbert Henry, b. Bermondsey, London, e. Camberwell, London, r. Bermondsey, London, 11767, Private

BARRY, Albert Harold, b. Rotherhithe, London, e. Deptford, London, r. Rotherhithe, London, 12018, Private (formerly 13456, Duke of Cornwall's Light Infantry)

BARTLETT, Reginald, b. Christchurch, Hants, e. Christchurch, Hants, r. Springbourne, Hants, 3/3672, Private

BATTLEY, Henry George, b. Walworth, London, e. Holborn, London, r. Battersea, London, 11750, Private (formerly 12568, Duke of Cornwall's Light Infantry)

BENBOW, Samuel Henry, b. Aston, Birmingham, e. Birmingham, r. Aston, Birmingham, 11743, Private (formerly 12644, Duke of Cornwall's Light Infantry)

BESANT, Arthur John, b. Leytonstone, Essex, e. Stratford, Essex, r. Leyton, Essex, 11748, Private (formerly 15602, Duke of Cornwall's Light Infantry)

BIBBEY, John Thomas, b. Hackney, London, e. Finsbury Barracks, London, r. Homerton, London, 12011, L/Cpl (formerly 13448, Duke of Cornwall's Light Infantry)

BILLINGS, Thomas Brown, b. Belton, Rutland, e. Stratford, Essex, r. Leytonstone, Essex, 16246, Private

BLACKBURN, Harry George, b. Guildford, Surrey, e. Romsey, Hants, r. Andover, Hants, 10825, Private

BOLSTER, Edgar Henry, b. Stoke Trister, Somerset, e. Alton, Hants, r. Bentley, Hants, 6341, Private

BRAY, William, b. Hertford, Herts, e. Holloway, London, r. Camden Town, London, 16193, Private

BREWER, Ernest, b. Cranbourne, Dorset, e. Bournemouth, Hants, r. Upper Parkstone, Dorset, 15858, Private

BRIDLE, James, b. Blandford, Dorset, e. Bournemouth, Hants, 15866, Private

BROOKS, William Henry, b. Easton, Hants, e. Winchester, Hants, r. Sutton Scotney, Hants, 10475, Private

BROWN, Sidney, b. West End, Southampton, e. Southampton, 10733, Private

BROWN, William James, b. Hackney, London, e. Poplar, London, r. Millwall, London, 15965, Private (formerly 18815, Duke of Cornwall's Light Infantry)

BUCKLE, George William, b. Southampton, Hants, e. Southampton, Hants, 10732, Private

BULL, Cecil, b. Carisbrooke, IOW, e. Newport, IOW, 10979, Private

CAINE, James, b. Smethwick, e. Birmingham, 11772, Private (formerly 12940, Duke of Cornwall's Light Infantry)

CAMFIELD, Alfred, b. Islington, London, e. Holloway, London, 16191, Private

CANNONS, Frederick Charles, b. East Tytherley, Hants, e. Romsey, Hants, r. East Tytherley, Hants, 10838, Private

CARTER, George Victor, b. Sholing, Hants, e. Southampton, Hants, r. Willesden, London, 10571, Private

CHALMERS, Robert, b. Lambeth, London, e. London, r. Wandsworth, London, 11778, Private (formerly 13731, Duke of Cornwall's Light Infantry)

CLARKE, Frederick Bert, b. Washwood Heath, Birmingham, e. Birmingham, r. Nechells, Birmingham, 11773, Private (formerly 13081, Duke of Cornwall's Light Infantry)

CLARKE, Whitmore, b. Sedgeley, Staffs, e. Birmingham, r. Bidford-on-Avon, Warwick, 11788, Cpl

COLLINS, Albert, b. Rogate, Sussex, e. Aldershot, Hants, r. Liss, Hants, 10583, Private

COOK, Alan, b. Great Tey, Essex, e. Winchester, Hants, r. Great Tey, Essex, 10983, Private

COSTER, Edward Edwin, b. Amport, Andover, Hants, e. Andover, Hants, 10834, Private

COWAN, Alfred, b. Westminster, London, e. Caxton Hall, London, r. Edgware Road, London, 11780, Private (formerly 13742, Duke of Cornwall's Light Infantry)

CRESSWELL, John, b. St James, Southampton, e. Southampton, 10938, Private

CROUTEAR, John, b. Fawley, Hants, e. Southampton, r. Fawley, Hants, 10745, Private

CURTIS, Frederick, b. West End, Southampton, Hants, e. Southampton, r. West End, Southampton, 10747, Private

CURTIS, George Henry, b. West End, Southampton, Hants, e. Southampton, r. West End, Southampton, 10743, Private

DALY, Frank, b. Walworth, London, e. Southwark, London, r. Newington Butts, London, 12024, Private

DANIEL, Charles William, b. Poplar, London, e. Winchester, Hants, r. East Ham, Essex, 9641, Private

DANIELS, Frank, b. Lawford, Hants, e. Bournemouth, Hants, r. Lower Kingstone, Hants, 10843, Private

DENHAM, James Alfred, b. Fair Oak, Hants, e. Winchester, Hants, r. Horton Heath, Hants, 10845, Private

DOPE, Harold Frank, b. Southampton, Hants, e. Southampton, 10750, Private

DRAKE, William Henry, b. Bentley, Hants, e. Romsey, Hants, r. East Tytherley, Hants, 11051, Private

DRISCOLL, Albert Joseph, b. Portsmouth, Hants, e. Portsmouth, r. Portsea, Hants, 3/4738, Sgt

DUFFIN, Harry George, b. Horton Heath, Hants, e. Basingstoke, Hants, r. Horton Heath, Hants, 10846, Private

EDMONDS, Harry, b. St Maurice, Winchester, e. Southampton, r. St Denys, Southampton, 3/4734, Sgt

ELLIS, Albert Edward, b. Mile End, London, e. London, r. Lowneld Heath, Sussex, 11809, Private (formerly 12512, Duke of Cornwall's Light Infantry)

EMERY, George, b. Shirley, Hants, e. Southampton, Hants, r. Bitterne Park, Southampton, 10943, Private

EVANS, Albert Henry, b. St Mary's, Birmingham, e. Birmingham, 11798, Private (formerly 13906, Duke of Cornwall's Light Infantry)

EVANS, Ernest, b. Wolverhampton, Staffs, e. Birmingham, r. Handsworth, Staffs, 16050, Private (formerly 18980, Duke of Cornwall's Light Infantry)

EVES, Edwin, b. Portsmouth, Hants, e. Portsmouth, 10626, Private

FLAVELL, Stanley Arthur, b. Northfield, Birmingham, e. Birmingham, 11800, Private

FLUX, George Henry, b. St John's, Winchester, Hants, e. Winchester, 3/4515, Sgt

FLYNN, Edward Thomas, b. Chatham, Kent, e. Portsmouth, Hants, r. Pittsmoor, Sheffield, 6794, Private

FOMES, James Samuel, b. All Saints, Birmingham, e. Birmingham, 11757, Private (formerly 13943, Duke of Cornwall's Light Infantry)

FULLBROOK, Frederick, b. Wokingham, Berks, e. Hartley Wintney, Hants, r. Wokingham, Berks, 15902, Private

GALLEY, George, b. Great Tey, Essex, e. Winchester, Hants, r. Great Tey, Essex, 10991, Private

GALLOP, Harold, b. Lake, IOW, e. Newport, IOW, 10855, Private

GLADDIS, Albert Henry, b. Atherfields, IOW, e. Newport, IOW, r. Upper Appleford, IOW, 10857, Private

GORMAN, Frederick Thomas, b. Aldershot, Hants, e. Co Kildare, r. Wicklow, 17542, Private

GOUCHER, James Harvey, b. Copythorne, Hants, e. Southampton, Hants, r. Copythorne, Hants, 10764, Private

GRANT, William, b. Spike Island, Co Cork, e. Southampton, r. Atcliff, Kent, 10761, L/Cpl

GRIFFITHS, Alfred, b. Old Ford, London, e. Bow, London, 11818, Private

HALL, William Dennis, b. Milton, Northants, e. Southampton, r. Northampton, 10945, Private

HANNAFORD, George, b. St Pancras, London, e. London, r. Westminster, London, 11842, Private (formerly 14235, Duke of Cornwall's Light Infantry)

HARDY, George, b. Limehouse, London, e. Poplar, London, r. Limehouse, London, 11845, Private (formerly 14310, Duke of Cornwall's Light Infantry)

HARFIELD, Montague John, b. Winchester, Hants, e. Winchester, r. Sutton Scotney, Hants, 10466, Private

HARPER, Thomas Harold, b. Islington, London, e. London, r. Newtown, Montgomery, 10861, L/Cpl

HARRIS, Benjamin James Thomas, b. Acocks Green, Warks, e. Birmingham, r. Castle Bromwich, Warks, 12027, Private (formerly 14346, Duke of Cornwall's Light Infantry)

HARRIS, Frank Thomas, b. St George's Birmingham, e. Birmingham, 11824, Private (formerly 13095, Duke of Cornwall's Light Infantry)

HICKS, George Thomas, b. Kensington, London, e. Marylebone, London, r. Ladbroke Grove London, 16019, Private (formerly 18930, Duke of Cornwall's Light Infantry)

HICKS, Harry William, b. Kensington, London, e. City of London, r. Vauxhall, London, 11847, Private (formerly 14318, Duke of Cornwall's Light Infantry)

HILL, George Leonard, b. Rotherhithe, London, e. Deptford, London, r. Rotherhithe, London, 11844, Private (formerly 14491, Duke of Cornwall's Light Infantry)

HILL, Percy, b. Aldershot, Hants, e. Birmingham, 11840, Private (formerly 12850, Duke of Cornwall's Light Infantry)

HILLARY, Edwin George, b. Micheldever, Hants, e. Winchester, Hants, r. Sutton Scotney, Hants, 10470, Private

HILLARY, Victor Frederick, b. Hunton, Hants, e. Winchester, Hants, r. Sutton Scotney, Hants, 10477, Private

HIRONS, Albert, b. Ladywood, Birmingham, e. Birmingham, 11828, Private

HOARE, Ernest, b. Abbotts Ann, Hants, e. Andover, Hants, r. Ramridge, Hants, 10998, Private

HOBDAY, John, b. Liverpool, e. London, r. Allerton, Lancs, 16259, Private

HOBDAY, William John, b. King's Heath, Birmingham, e. Birmingham, 11832, Private (formerly 14434, Duke of Cornwall's Light Infantry)

HOBIN, Charles William, b. Blackfriars, London, e. Wandsworth, London, r. Battersea, London, 11835, Private (formerly 14436, Duke of Cornwall's Light Infantry)

HODDER, Thomas George, b. Lyme Regis, Dorset, e. Southampton, Hants r. Freemantle, Hants, 10605, Cpl

HODGES, Howard Frederick, b. Winson Green, Warks, e. Birmingham, 11829, Private

HOLLIS, Reginald, b. Newport, IOW, e. Newport, IOW, 10863, Private

HOOKEY, Henry, b. St James, Bournemouth, Hants, e. Bournemouth, 15891, Private

HOWARD, William, b. Islington, London, e. Holloway, London, 16247, Private

HOWE, William, b. Milden, Suffolk, e. Winchester, Hants, r. Chappel, Essex, 11002, Private

HOWES, Fred, b. Bournemouth, Hants, e. Deptford, London, r. Rotherhithe, London, 11836, Private (formerly 14465, Duke of Cornwall's Light Infantry)

HUGHES, Herbert, b. Edgbaston, Warks, e. Birmingham, 11846, Private (formerly 14315, Duke of Cornwall's Light Infantry)

HUMPHRIES, James Charles, b. St Pancras, London, e. Southwark, London, r. Newington, London, 11843, Private

HUNNYBUN, William, b. Carisbrooke, IOW, e. Newport, IOW, 10999, Private

HUNT, Charles Henry, b. Moseley, Worcs, e. Birmingham, 11826, Private (formerly 13708, Duke of Cornwall's Light Infantry)

HURLOCK, William, b. Ashe, Hants, e. Alton, Hants, r. Binstead, Hants, 6422, L/Cpl

IRONS, Alfred Richard, b. Castle Bromwich, Warks, e. Birmingham, r. Castle Bromwich, 11852, Private (formerly 13093, Duke of Cornwall's Light Infantry)

JOHNSON, Ernest, b. Wandsworth, London, e. Town Hall, Walham Green, London, r. Fulham, London, 11854, Private (formerly 14515, Duke of Cornwall's Light Infantry)

JONES, Albert, b. Shoreditch, London, e. Barking, Essex, r. Shoreditch, London, 12004, Private (formerly 14510, Duke of Cornwall's Light Infantry)

JURD, Frederick, b. West End, Southampton, Hants e. Southampton, r. West End, Southampton, 10772, Private

KEMPTON, Charles, b. Burton-on-Trent, Staffs, e. Shepherd's Bush, London, 12091, Private

KENDALL, William, b. Ripley, Christchurch, Hants, e. Ringwood, Hants, r. Shirley, Hants, 10507, Private

KENNARD, Reginald James, b. Gosport, Hants, e. Portsmouth, Hants, r. Gosport, 10636, Private

KING, Leonard Lane, b. Magdalene Laver, Essex, e. Islington, London, r. North Weald, Essex, 11863, Private (formerly 14610, Duke of Cornwall's Light Infantry)

KNIGHT, Charles, b. Hedge End, Hants, e. Southampton, Hants, r. Bitterne, Hants, 10776, Private

KNIGHT, Charles Frederick, b. Surbiton, Surrey, e. Basingstoke, Hants, 10874, Private

KNODLER, Frederick Charles, b. Bermondsey, London, e. Southampton, r. Maidenhead, Berks, 10568, Cpl

LACE, Albert Thomas, b. Bermondsey, London, e. London, r. Rotherhithe, London, 11878, Private (formerly 12733, Duke of Cornwall's Light Infantry)

LAIGHT, Francis Stewart, b. King's Heath, Warks, e. King's Heath, r. Birmingham, 11866, Private (formerly 12658, Duke of Cornwall's Light Infantry)

LANE, Arthur George, b. Islington, London, e. London, r. Kentish Town, London, 11877, Private (formerly 12519, Duke of Cornwall's Light Infantry)

LARKIN, Algernon, b. Rotherhithe, London, e. Deptford, London, 16087, Private (formerly 19946, Duke of Cornwall's Light Infantry)

LEIGHTON, Lawrence, b. Walthamstow, Essex, e. Caxton Hall, London, r. Forest Gate, Essex, 11867, Private (formerly 13180, Duke of Cornwall's Light Infantry)

LIGHT, Bertie James, b. West End, Southampton, Hants, e. Southampton, r. West End, Southampton, 10954, Private

LIGHT, Walter, b. West End, Southampton, Hants, e. Southampton, r. West End, Southampton, 10779, Private

LLOYD, Ernest William, b. Forest Gate, Essex, e. Holloway, London, r. Stoke Newington, London, 16222, Private

LODER, Arthur, b. Waltham Abbey, Essex, e. Stratford, Essex, r. Waltham Abbey, Essex, 11874, Private (formerly 14666, Duke of Cornwall's Light Infantry)

LOFTIN, Ernest John, b. Notting Hill, London, e. Holloway, London, r. Islington, London, 16208, Private

MAHONEY, Ernest, b. Stratford, Essex, e. Stratford, Essex, r. Old Ford, London, 16201, Private

MARKS, James, b. Millbrook, Hants, e. Winchester, Hants, r. Allbrook, Hants, 4983, Private

MARTIN, William, b. Poltimore, Devon, e. Bodmin, Cornwall, r. Lewame, Cornwall, 11891, Private (formerly 13316, Duke of Cornwall's Light Infantry)

MATTHEWS, Thomas, b. Newport, IOW, e. Newport, IOW, 10884, Private

McCROSSEN, Edward George, b. Bermondsey, London, e. Camberwell, London, r. Blockley, London, 11883, Private (formerly 14920, Duke of Cornwall's Light Infantry)

McDERMOTT, Harry, b. Lambeth, London, e. Lambeth, London, r. Brixton, London, 11896, Private (formerly 14896, Duke of Cornwall's Light Infantry)

MELHUISH, Thomas, b. Langport, Somerset, e. Southampton, Hants, 3/4562, Private

MERNIN, Philip John, b. Westminster, London, e. London, r. Camden Town, London, 11884, Private (formerly 14127, Duke of Cornwall's Light Infantry)

MERRITT, Gilbert George, b. Shedfield, Hants, e. Southampton, Hants, r. Bishops Waltham, Hants, 10610, Private

MORGAN, Leonard James, b. Stepney, London, e. Caxton Hall, London, r. Ilford, Essex, 11879, Private (formerly 13160, Duke of Cornwall's Light Infantry)

MORRIS, William Henry, b. Kingsheath, Worcs, e. Birmingham, r. Kingsheath, Worcs, 11895, Private (formerly 14883, Duke of Cornwall's Light Infantry)

MOULD, George, b. Birmingham, e. Birmingham, 11889, Private (formerly 14963, Duke of Cornwall's Light Infantry)

NOLAN, James Patrick, b. Liverpool, e. London, r. Aldershot, Hants, 17780, Private

NUNN, James, b. Stepney, London, e. St Paul's Churchyard, London, r. Stepney, London, 16283, Private

NUNN, Thomas Benjamin, b. St Pancras, London, e. London, r. Islington, London, 11904, Private (formerly 12517, Duke of Cornwall's Light Infantry)

OSBORNE, William John, b. Stepney, London, e. Stratford, Essex, 15871, Private

OVERREE, Frederick Alfred, b. Whitechapel, London, e. Bow, London, 11910, Private

(formerly 15247, Duke of Cornwall's Light Infantry)

PALMER, William, b. Cobham, Kent, e. Southampton, Hants, 16210, Private

PARKIN, William, b. Potton, Beds, e. Southampton, Hants, r. Romsey, Hants, 10961, Private

PEARCE, Joseph, b. Bethnal Green, London, e. Westminster, London, r. Hackney, London, 12029, Private

PEIRCE, Charles Walter, b. Newport, IOW, e. Newport, IOW, r. Barton Village, IOW, 10896, Private

PEMBERTON, Reuben, b. Haverton Hill, Durham, e. Stockton-on-Tees, Durham, r. Haverton Hill, Durham, 11015, Private

PENNY, Dennis, b. Southampton, Hants, e. Southampton, r. Millbrook, Hants, 10963, Private

PERCIVAL, Fred, b. Great Tey, Essex, e. Winchester, Hants, r. Great Tey, Essex, 11016, Private

PETTIFER, Ernest, b. Cropredy, Oxon, e. Birmingham, r. Cropredy, Oxon, 12021, Private (formerly 14827, Duke of Cornwall's Light Infantry)

PHILLIPS, Percy, b. Stoke Newington, Middx, e. Holborn, London, r. Dulwich, London, 11922, Private (formerly 14750, Duke of Cornwall's Light Infantry)

PIPER, Sidney, b. Hartley Wintney, Hants, e. Aldershot, Hants, r. Winchfield, Hants, 10589, A/Cpl

POTTER, Charles Frederick, b. Stepney, London, e. St Paul's Churchyard, London, r. Stepney, London, 16281, Private

PRATLEY, Frederick Walter, b. Leafield, Oxon, e. Birmingham, r. Witney, Oxon, 11911, Private (formerly 12647, Duke of Cornwall's Light Infantry)

PRICE, Edward, b. Winson Green, Warks, e. Birmingham, r. Handsworth, Staffs, 11921, Private (formerly 14853, Duke of Cornwall's Light Infantry)

PROWSE, Walter Henry, b. Exeter, e. Holloway, London, r. Paignton, Devon, 16071, Private (formerly 19010, Duke of Cornwall's Light Infantry)

PRYKE, Percy Wilfred, b. Stowmarket, Suffolk, e. Winchester, Hants, r. Bury St Edmunds, Suffolk, 11018, Private

PURSE, Henry John, b. Hornsey, Middx, e. St Pancras, London, r. Kentish Town, London, 11993, Private (formerly 14858, Duke of Cornwall's Light Infantry)

RAYNOR, William, b. Portsmouth, Hants, e. Kingsway, London, r. Paddington, London, 16223, Private

READ, Henry Arthur Charles, b. Winchester, Hants, e. Southampton, Hants, r. Shirley, Hants, 10249, Private

REEVES, Arthur Harry, b. Shirley, Hants, e. Southampton, Hants, r. Shirley, Hants, 10215, Private

REMES, Percy, b. Stonehouse, Glos, e. Winchester, Hants, 7384, Private

RICHES, Arthur Henry, b. Canning Town, Essex, e. Canning Town, Essex, 11994, Private (formerly 15173, Duke of Cornwall's Light Infantry)

ROBERTS, Richard, b. Finsbury, London, e. St Pancras, London, r. King's Cross, London, 11929, Private (formerly 15223, Duke of Cornwall's Light Infantry)

ROBINSON, William George, b. Winson Green, Warks, e. Birmingham, 11928, Private (formerly 12662, Duke of Cornwall's Light Infantry)

ROUND, Horace Vernon Grant, b. Ladywood, Warks, e. Birmingham, 11920, Private (formerly 15192, Duke of Cornwall's Light Infantry)

ROWE, Harold, b. North Stoneham, Hants, e. Southampton, Hants, r. Stoneham, Hants, 10966, Private

SALMON, Herbert Joshua, b. Harbridge, Hants, e. Ringwood, Hants, r. Ringwood, Hants, 10904, L/Cpl

SAUNDERS, Williams, b. Homerton, London, e. Stratford, Essex, r. Homerton, London, 11947, Private (formerly 15084, Duke of Cornwall's Light Infantry)

SCHOFIELD, George James, b. Camberwell, London, e. St Paul's Churchyard, London, r. Mitcham, Surrey, 11952, Private (formerly 15065, Duke of Cornwall's Light Infantry)

SCIVIER, Frederick, b. Wandsworth, London, e. Holborn, London, r. Tooting, London, 11946, Private (formerly 15126, Duke of Cornwall's Light Infantry)

SHEPPARD, Jack, b. Fulham, London, e. Fulham, London, 11930, Private (formerly 15135, Duke of Cornwall's Light Infantry)

SHUTTLEWORTH, Thomas Frederick, b. St Paul's, Birmingham, e. Birmingham, 11938, Private (formerly 15131, Duke of Cornwall's Light Infantry)

SILLENCE, William Henry, b. Romsey, Hants, e. Southampton, Hants, r. Upton Grey, Hants, 10793, Private

SIMMS, Arthur George, b. Oxford, e. Hounslow, Middx, 15983, Private (formerly 18849, Duke of Cornwall's Light Infantry)

SKETCHLEY, Frederick, b. Hockley, Warks, e. Birmingham, 11944, Private (formerly 15004, Duke of Cornwall's Light Infantry)

SLATER, William James, b. King's Lynn, Norfolk, e. St Pancras, London, r. King's Lynn, Norfolk, 11941, Cpl (formerly 12488, Duke of Cornwall's Light Infantry)

SLATIER, William, b. Southwark, London, e. Southwark, London, 11931, Private (formerly 15097, Duke of Cornwall's Light Infantry)

SMELT, George, b. Regent's Park, London, e. Birmingham, r. Handsworth, Warks, 11943, Private (formerly 13026, Duke of Cornwall's Light Infantry)

SMETH, Frank, b. Bournemouth, Hants, e. Weybridge, Surrey, r. Bournemouth, 11516, L/Cpl

SPEARINK, Frederick, b. Kensington, London, e.

Lambeth, London, r. Mitcham, Surrey, 11945, Private (formerly 15020, Duke of Cornwall's Light Infantry)

STANTON, George, b. Hoxton, London, e. Holloway, London, r. Islington, London, 15859, Private

STOKES, Ernest, b. Greatham, Hants, e. Aldershot, Hants, r. Greatham, Hants, 10491, Private

STURNEY, George, b. Guildford, Surrey, e. East Ham, Essex, r. New Malden, Surrey, 11025, L/Cpl

TAYLOR, Hubert Francis Walter, b. Holbrook, Hants, e. Brockenhurst, Hants, r. Lyndhurst Road, Hants, 16148, Private

THATCHOR, Alfred James, b. Sherborne-St-John, Hants, e. Basingstoke, Hants, r. Sherborne-St-John, Hants, 11069, L/Cpl

THOMPSON, Benjamin Herbert, b. Holborn, London, e. London, r. Kingsway, London, 12012, Private

THOMPSON, Frederick Arthur, b. West End, Southampton, Hants, e. Southampton, r. West End, Southampton, 10800, Private

TIDY, William, b. Stepney, London, e. Stratford, Essex, r. Forest Gate, Essex, 11969, Private (formerly 15623, Duke of Cornwall's Light Infantry)

TONGS, Henry, b. Romsey, Hants, c. Southampton, Hants, r. Romsey, Hants, 10801, Private

TOOGOOD, George, b. Shorwell, IOW, e. Newport, IOW, r. Chale, IOW, 10908, Private

TOOGOOD, Herbert, b. Carisbrooke, IOW, e. Newport, IOW, r. Chale, IOW, 10909, Cpl

TROUT, William Charles, b. Camberwell, London, e. Camberwell, London, 11967, Private (formerly 15342, Duke of Cornwall's Light Infantry)

VYE, Alfred, b. Upham, Hants, e. Southampton, Hants, r. Upham, Hants, 10609, Private

WADMORE, William, b. Godshill, IOW, e. Ryde, IOW, r. Briddlesford Lodge Cottage, nr Wootton, IOW, 10723, Private

WALDER, Alfred, b. Scanes Hill, Sussex, e. Bordon, Hants, r. Petersfield, Hants, 15895, Private

WEBB, Albert Lewis, b. Lockerley, Hants, e. Romsey, Hants, r. Tytherley, Hants, 10918, Private

WEBB, Leonard, b. West End, Southampton, Hants, e. Southampton, r. West End, Southampton, 10804, Private

WELLS, Harold, b. All Saints, Birmingham, e. Birmingham, 11987, Private (formerly 15635, Duke of Cornwall's Light Infantry)

WELLSTEAD, Edwin, b. Curdridge, Hants, e. Southampton, Hants, r. Curdridge, Hants, 10805, Private

WELLSTEAD, Robert Henry, b. Wellow, IOW, e. Yarmouth, IOW, 11036, Private

WHEELER, Allan, b. Peebles, e. Birmingham, r. Nailsea, Somerset, 11980, L/Cpl (formerly 13092, Duke of Cornwall's Light Infantry)

WHITCHER, William, b. New Milton, Hants, e. Bournemouth, Hants, r. New Milton, Hants, 10454, Private

WHITE, Walter James, b. St Helen's, Ryde, IOW, e. Ryde, IOW, r. Oakfield, IOW, 11115, Private

WHITEHORNE, Frank Alexander, b. Over Wallop, Hants, e. Southampton, Hants, r. Winchester, Hants, 10808, Private

WILD, James, b. Stepney, London, e. Canning Town, Essex, r. Stepney, London, 11996, Private (formerly 15651, Duke of Cornwall's Light Infantry)

WILLIAMS, Albert, b. Broughton, Hants, e. Southampton, Hants, r. Broughton, Hants, 10809, Private

WILLIAMS, Charles, b. Chillerton, IOW, e. Newport, IOW, r. Gunville, IOW, 11033, Private

WILLIAMS, Henry Thomas, b. Tottenham, London, e. Stratford, Essex, 15933, Private (formerly 18721, Duke of Cornwall's Light Infantry)

WILLS, Arthur Edward, b. Poplar, London, e. Finsbury Barracks, London, r. Poplar, London, 11985, Private (formerly 15657, Duke of Cornwall's Light Infantry)

WOLF, Charles Frank, b. Newport, IOW, e. Newport, IOW, 11116, Private

WREN, Alfred, b. Millbrook, Hants, e. Southampton, Hants, r. Shirleywarren, Hants, 10807, Private

WRIGHT, John Frederick, b. Islington, London, e. Hampstead, London, r. Highbury, London, 11981, Cpl (formerly 12569, Duke of Cornwall's Light Infantry)

YOUNG, Charles Bertram, b. Newport, IOW, e. Newport, IOW, 10919, Private

YOUNG, James, b. Bitterne, Hants, e. Southampton, Hants, r. Bitterne, Hants, 10815, Private

YOUNG, Reginald Henry, b. St Mary's, Southampton, Hants, e. Southampton, 10229, Private

The Lancashire Fusiliers – 1st Battalion

BROMLEY, Cuthbert, Temp Major, VC

ASHWORTH, Albert, b. Gt Harwood, Lancs, e. Accrington, Lancs, r. Gt Harwood, 6232, Private

BACON, Jonathan, b. Liverpool, e. Manchester, 4869, Private

CARNEY, Patrick, b. Ashton-in-Makerfield, Lancs, e. Wigan, Lancs, 5261, Private

CARROLL, Matthew, b. Wigan, Lancs, e. Wigan, 5260, Private

COOK, Harry Thompson, b. Bastwell, Blackburn, Lancs, e. Blackburn, Lancs, 2976, Private

CRUSE, William, b. Blackpool, Lancs, e. Bury, Lancs, r. Blackpool, 688, Private

DAW, Andrew, b. Rawtenstall, Lancs, e. Bury, Lancs, r. Rochdale, Lancs, 4440, Private

FARRELL, Michael, b. Manchester, e. Manchester, 4751, Private

FLETCHER, Robert, b. Skerton, Lancs, e. Manchester, 3267, Private

GROGAN, Francis, b. Preston, Lancs, e. Adlington, Lancs, r. Barrow-in-Furness, Lancs, 21158, Private

HAGAN, Arthur, b. Bootle, Lancs, e. Warrington, Lancs, r. Liverpool, 9814, Private

HOUGH, Robert, b. Preston, Lancs, e. Preston, 8856, Private

HUGHES, John, b. Salford, Lancs, e. Bury, Lancs, 4599, Private

MCCONVILLE, Arthur, b. Burnley, Lancs, c. Burnley, 4964, L/Cpl

MCCORMICK, William, b. Rawtenstall, Lancs, e. Bury, Lancs, 9614, Private

MCDONOUGH, Andrew, b. Wigan, Lancs, e. Sunderland, Durham, 13661, Private

MCFEELEY, John, b. Dublin, e. Bury, Lancs, 2457, Private

MCGUIRE, Thomas, b. Parr, St Helens, Lancs, e. St Helens, 7537, Private

MCHUGH, John, b. Rochdale, Lancs, e. Bury, Lancs, r. Rochdale, 4629, Private

RIGBY, John, b. Walkden, Lancs, c. Bury, Lancs, r. Swinton, Lancs, 1831, Private

ROUNSWELL, Arthur, b. Manchester, e. Manchester, 5768, Private

STELL, Charles, b. Skipton, Yorks, e. Manchester, 8179, Private

STEVENS, William Robert, b. Paddington, Middx, e. Hounslow, Middx, 2669, Private

TOVEY, Edward Alfred, b. Birmingham, e. Birmingham, 731, Private

WHITESIDE, John, b. Blackburn, Lancs, e. Bury, Lancs, 9798, Private

WILLIAMS, Brinley, b. Tredegar, Mon, e. Brynmawr, Brecknock, 18455, Private

WILSON, Alfred, b. Huyton, Liverpool, e. Seaforth, Lancs, 7079, Private

The Essex Regiment – 1st Battalion

CASSWELL, Frederick Charles, 2/Lt (TP), (att'd Essex Reg), Bedfordshire Regiment, 10th Battalion

RIDDELL, Frederick James, Lt (TP), (att'd Essex Reg), Bedfordshire Regiment, 9th Battalion

ADCOCK, John, b. Saham Toney, Norfolk, e. Norwich, r. Saham Toney, 20584, Private (formerly 17972, Norfolk Regiment)

ALEXANDER, Dennis, b. Long Stratton, Norfolk, e. Norwich, r. Long Stratton, 20564, L/Cpl (formerly 17909, Norfolk Regiment)

ALLEN, Dennis, b. Hellifield, Yorks, e. Norwich, r. Saxlingham, Norfolk, 20704, Private (formerly 17610, Norfolk Regiment)

ALLERTON, Reuben, b. Littleport, Cambs, e. Norwich, r. Wisbech, Cambs, 20586, Private (formerly 8860, Norfolk Regiment)

ALLSOP, Robert William, b. Lakenheath, Suffolk, e. Norwich, r. Ringstead, Norfolk, 20733, Private (formerly 17673, Norfolk Regiment)

AMIS, Arthur Abraham, b. Potter Heigham, Norfolk, e. Great Yarmouth, Norfolk, r. Great Yarmouth, 20548, Private (formerly 17803, Norfolk Regiment)

ANDREWS, George Frederick, b. Bermondsey, Surrey, e. Great Yarmouth, Norfolk, r. Gorleston-on-Sea, Norfolk, 20640, Private (formerly 16486, Norfolk Regiment)

ANDREWS, Robert Charles, b. Swainsthorpe, Norfolk, e. Norwich, r. Kirstead, Norfolk, 20641, Private (formerly 17717, Norfolk Regiment)

APPLEGATE, Frederick George, b. East Ham, Essex, e. Wimbledon, Surrey, r. Wimbledon, 20539, Private (formerly 17842, Norfolk Regiment)

ASHBY, George Stanley, b. King's Lynn, Norfolk, e. Norwich, r. King's Lynn, 20585, Private (formerly 18019, Norfolk Regiment)

AVIS, Sidney, b. West Hartlepool, Durham, e. Norwich, r. Pentney, Norfolk, 20580, Private (formerly 17764, Norfolk Regiment)

BAILEY, George William, b. Browston, Suffolk, e. Dunbar, r. Gorleston-on-Sea, 20589, Private (formerly 11461, Norfolk Regiment)

BARNES, Frederick George, b. Shoreditch, Middx, e. Shoreditch, r. Haggerston, Middx, 20587, Private (formerly 17761, Norfolk Regiment)

BARNES, Ralph, b. North Walsham, Norfolk, e. Norwich, r. North Walsham, 20588, Private (formerly 18436, Norfolk Regiment)

BENIFER, Arthur, b. Congham, Norfolk, e. Norwich, r. Wimbotsham, Norfolk, 20645, Private (formerly 17655, Norfolk Regiment)

BENNINGTON, Edgar, b. Melton, Norfolk, e. Norwich, r. Easton, Norwich, 20593, Private (formerly 17857, Norfolk Regiment)

BERRY, Albert, b. West Lynn, Norfolk, e. Norwich, r. Middleton, Norfolk, 20649, Private (formerly 17583, Norfolk Regiment)

BERRY, Guy, b. East Dereham, Norfolk, e. Norwich, r. Leyton, Essex, 20634, A/Cpl (formerly 3/6759, Norfolk Regiment)

BLACKBURN, Alfred, b. Brancaster, Norfolk, e. Norwich, r. King's Lynn, Norfolk, 20712, Private (formerly 12157, Norfolk Regiment)

BLAKE, Frederick George, b. Rockland St Mary, Norfolk, e. Norwich, r. Rockland St Mary, 20590, L/Cpl (formerly 9327, Norfolk Regiment)

BLOWER, Wilfred, b. Saham Toney, Norfolk, e. Norwich, r. Saham Toney, 20592, Private (formerly 17976, Norfolk Regiment)

BOGGIS, John William, b. South Lopham, Norfolk, e. Norwich, r. Diss, Norfolk, 20648, Private (formerly 18438, Norfolk Regiment)

BOUGHEN, Philip, b. Walpole St Peter, Norfolk, e. Norwich, r. Terrington St Clements, Norfolk, 20647, Private (formerly 17612, Norfolk Regiment)

BRIGHT, Arthur James, b. Houghton, Norfolk, e.

Norwich, r. Houghton, 20814, Private (formerly 17668, Norfolk Regiment)

BRISTOW, Frederick, b. Old Catton, Norfolk, e. Norwich, r. Old Catton, 20716, Private (formerly 17273, Norfolk Regiment)

BROWN, George Lambert, b. Holloway, Middx, e. Norwich, r. Wymondham, Norfolk, 20642, Private (formerly 17513, Norfolk Regiment)

BROWN, James Charles, b. East Walton, Norfolk, e. Norwich, r. Marham, Norfolk, 20646, Private (formerly 17532, Norfolk Regiment)

BROWNE, Walter George, b. Pewsey, Wilts, e. Woolwich, Kent, r. Forest Gate, Essex, 20643, Private (formerly 17379, Norfolk Regiment)

BRUMMETT, Albert, b. Stratford, Essex, e. Norwich, r. Norwich, 20686, L/Cpl (formerly 10215, Norfolk Regiment)

BUNTING, Frederick Henry, b. Postwick, Norfolk, e. Norwich, r. Whitewell, Norfolk, 20591, Private (formerly 17915, Norfolk Regiment)

BUTTERS, Edward John, b. Beechamwell, Norfolk, e. Norwich, r. Beechamwell, 20578, Private (formerly 17843, Norfolk Regiment)

CARTER, James Henry, b. Great Yarmouth, Norfolk, e. Great Yarmouth, r. Great Yarmouth, 20653, Private (formerly 9428, Norfolk Regiment)

CATTERMOLE, Richard Stephen, b. Southwark, Surrey, e. Wimbledon, Surrey, r. Raynes Park, Surrey, 20595, Private (formerly 18009, Norfolk Regiment)

CAWSTON, Arthur, b. Middleton, Norfolk, e. Norwich, r. Wormegay, Norfolk, 20638, L/Cpl (formerly 17584, Norfolk Regiment)

CHANNON, Albert Henry, b. Battersea, Surrey, c. Battersea, r. Battersea, 20596, Private (formerly 3/8006, Norfolk Regiment)

CHAPMAN, Raymond Lewis, b. North Heigham, Norfolk, e. Norwich, r. Norwich, 20724, Private (formerly 9098, Norfolk Regiment)

CLARE, James Percy, b. Alpington, Norfolk, e. Norwich, r. Framlingham Earl, Norfolk, 20651, Private (formerly 18613, Norfolk Regiment)

CLARKE, George, b. Scole, Norfolk, e. Leeds, r. Bruntcliffe, Leeds, 20706, Private (formerly 10125, Norfolk Regiment)

COMER, Harold, b. Ryburgh, Norfolk, e. Norwich, r. Great Ryburgh, Norfolk 20599, Private (formerly 17338, Norfolk Regiment)

COOTE, Frank Frederick, b. Steeple Bumpstead, Essex, e. Haverhill, Suffolk, r. Steeple Bumpstead, 20687, L/Cpl (formerly 8783, Norfolk Regiment)

CORDEROY, William, b. Lambeth, Surrey, e. Camberwell, Surrey, r. Lambeth, 20654, Private (formerly 17603, Norfolk Regiment)

CURD, Stephen, b. Bethnal Green, Middx, e. Shoreditch, Middx, r. Bethnal Green, 20600, Private (formerly 18007, Norfolk Regiment)

CURTIS, Bertram, b. Norwich, e. Norwich, r. Norwich, 20598, Private (formerly 17215, Norfolk Regiment)

DAVIDSON, Stanley, b. Aylsham, Norfolk, e. Norwich, r. Booton, Norfolk, 20602, Private (formerly 17773, Norfolk Regiment)

DAVIES, William, b. Westminster, Middx, e. Marylebone, Middx, r. Westminster, Middx, 20604, L/Cpl (formerly 10020, Norfolk Regiment)

DAVISON, Samuel, b. East Harling, Norfolk, e. Norwich, r. Kenninghall, Norfolk, 20551, Private (formerly 17865, Norfolk Regiment)

DEBBAGE, John Prindle, b. Ranworth, Norfolk, e. Norwich, r. Bramerton, Norfolk, 20655, Private (formerly 17652, Norfolk Regiment)

DISDLE, Reginald George, b. Saham Toney, Norfolk, e. Norwich, r. Watton, Norfolk, 20566, Private (formerly 17982, Norfolk Regiment)

DONGER, Thomas William, b. Kings Lynn, Norfolk, e. Norwich, r. King's Lynn, 20714, Private (formerly 17047, Norfolk Regiment)

DYBALL, Frederick, b. Westwick, Norwich, e. Norwich, r. Hickling, Norfolk, 20601, Private (formerly 17102, Norfolk Regiment)

DYBALL, Sydney, b. Beeston, Norfolk, e.

Norwich, r. Sheringham, Norfolk, 20656, Private (formerly 17674, Norfolk Regiment)

EDWARDS, John, b. Brandon, Suffolk, e. Norwich, r. Little Ellingham, Norfolk, 20553, Private (formerly 17711, Norfolk Regiment)

EMMS, Herbert Sidney, b. North Lopham, Norfolk, e. Norwich, r. North Lopham, 20661, Private (formerly 17447, Norfolk Regiment)

EVANS, George, b. Stepney, Middx, e. Shoreditch, Middx, r. Cambridge Heath, Middx, 20603, Private (formerly 17560, Norfolk Regiment)

EVERETT, Walter Charles, b. Southwark, Surrey, e. London, r. Southwark, 20689, L/Cpl (formerly 8126, Norfolk Regiment)

EWEN, Robert Edward, b. Sedgeford, Norfolk, e. Norwich, r. Heacham, Norfolk, 20660, Private (formerly 17538, Norfolk Regiment)

FAKE, Herbert, b. King's Lynn, e. Norwich, r. King's Lynn, 20659, Private (formerly 17732, Norfolk Regiment)

FARRER, Harry, b. Norwich, e. Norwich, r. Norwich, 20718, Private (formerly 6322, Norfolk Regiment)

FARROW, George Robert, b. Wymondham, Norfolk, e. Norwich, r. Wymondham, 20605, Private (formerly 17631, Norfolk Regiment)

FILBY, William Benjamin, b. Tilney All Saints, Norfolk, e. Norwich, r. Gorefield, Cambs, 20699, Private (formerly 18950, Norfolk Regiment)

FISHER, Thomas Alfred, b. St John's Wood, Middx, e. St Pancras, Middx, r. Kentish Town, Middx, 20657, Private (formerly 17759, Norfolk Regiment)

FLAXMAN, Herbert James, b. Trunch, Norfolk, e. Norwich, r. Trunch, 20547, Private (formerly 17815, Norfolk Regiment)

FOULGER, Sidney, b. Norwich, e. Norwich, r. Norwich, 20567, Private (formerly 17782, Norfolk Regiment)

FRARY, Eldred John, b. Walsingham, Norfolk, e. Norwich, r. Walsingham, 20552, Private (formerly 17921, Norfolk Regiment)

FROST, Lamonia, b. Hellesdon, Norfolk, e. Norwich, r. Upper Hellesdon, Norfolk, 20606, L/Cpl (formerly 3/8012, Norfolk Regiment)

FULLER, Albert Sydney, b. Trunch, Norfolk, e. Norwich, r. Trunch, 20549, Private (formerly 17818, Norfolk Regiment)

FULLER, George Herbert, b. Carleton Rode, Norfolk, e. Norwich, r. Carleton Rode, 20559, Private (formerly 17784, Norfolk Regiment)

FULLER, John Sayer, b. Toft Monks, Norfolk, e. Norwich, r. Norton Subcourse, Norfolk, 20582, Private (formerly 17819, Norfolk Regiment)

GARROD, Arthur, b. Mundford, Norfolk, e. Norwich, r. Mundford, 20663, Private (formerly 17735, Norfolk Regiment)

GIBBS, Edward, b. Hickling, Norfolk, e. Norwich, r. Hickling, 20685, L/Cpl (formerly 17104, Norfolk Regiment)

GOOCH, Arthur, b. Norwich, e. Norwich, r. Norwich, 20538, Private (formerly 17846, Norfolk Regiment)

GOWING, Reginald George, b. Trunch, Norfolk, e. Norwich, r. Pulham Market, Norfolk, 20665, L/Cpl (formerly 17701, Norfolk Regiment)

GREEN, Charles William, b. King's Lynn, e. Norwich, r. King's Lynn, 20534, A/Sgt (formerly 3/10235, Norfolk Regiment)

GREENACRE, Henry, b. Great Yarmouth, Norfolk, e. Norwich, r. Great Grimsby, 20691, Private (formerly 7249, Norfolk Regiment)

GREENWOOD, William, b. Great Yarmouth, Norfolk, e. Great Yarmouth, r. Great Yarmouth, 20664, Private (formerly 18510, Norfolk Regiment)

GROPPLER, Hubert, b. Stroud Green, Middx, e. Chichester, Sussex, r. Westcliff-on-Sea, Essex, 19029, Private

HAINES, Sidney, b. Bale, Norfolk, e. Norwich, r. Sharrington, Norfolk, 20569, Private (formerly 17789, Norfolk Regiment)

HAINES, Walter Robert, b. Burnham Overy, Norfolk, e. Norwich, r. Burnham Overy,

20554, Private (formerly 17823, Norfolk Regiment)

HARDY, Albert G., b. South Lynn, Norfolk, e. Norwich, r. King's Lynn, Norfolk, 20069, Private (formerly 17737, Norfolk Regiment)

HARRIS, John, b. Custom House, Essex, e. Woolwich, Kent, r. Custom House, 18698, Private

HARVEY, Albert Edward, b. Mundham, Norfolk, e. Norwich, r. Sizeland, Norfolk, 20579, Private (formerly 17790, Norfolk Regiment)

HARVEY, Walter, b. Newton, Norfolk, e. Ferry Hill, r. Ferry Hill, 20668, Private (formerly 16437, Norfolk Regiment)

HEMBURY, Frank Edward, b. Islington, Middx, e. St Pancras, Middx, r. Kentish Town, Middx, 20667, Private (formerly 17646, Norfolk Regiment)

HENDRY, Edward, b. Fakenham, Norfolk, e. Norwich, r. Fakenham, 20693, Private (formerly 12220, Norfolk Regiment)

HICKS, Alfred Albert, b. Hockwold, Norfolk, e. Norwich, r. Hockwold, 2061, Private (formerly 16650, Norfolk Regiment)

HIGGINS, Alfred Brooks, b. Melbourn, Cambs, e. Norwich, r. Hampton-on-Thames, Middx, 20611, L/Cpl (formerly 16784, Norfolk Regiment)

HOGGETT, Albert James, b. Threxton, Norfolk, e. Norwich, r. Threxton, 20571, Private (formerly 17926, Norfolk Regiment)

HOGGETT, Herbert, b. Hilborough, Norfolk, e. Norwich, r. Hilborough, 20574, Private (formerly 17925, Norfolk Regiment)

HOLMAN, Walter, b. Shipdham, Norfolk, e. Norwich, r. Shipdham, 20542, Private (formerly 17870, Norfolk Regiment)

MUGGINS, Hugh William, b. Margate, Kent, e. Great Yarmouth, Norfolk, r. Great Yarmouth, 20609, Private (formerly 7899, Norfolk Regiment)

HUMPHRYS, Charles, b. Deptford, Kent, e. East Ham, Essex, r. East Ham, 20608, Private (formerly 17251, Norfolk Regiment)

JARVIS, Charles, b. Dersingham, Norfolk, e. Norwich, r. Titchwell, Norfolk, 20682, Private (formerly 18796, Norfolk Regiment)

JAY, Robert, b. Smallburgh, Norfolk, e. Norwich, r. Smallburgh, 20546, Private (formerly 17798, Norfolk Regiment)

JEARY, Francis Jacob, b. Bawburgh, Norfolk, e. Norwich, r. Norwich, 20544, Private (formerly 17874, Norfolk Regiment)

JEARY, George Henry, b. Bawburgh, Norfolk, e. Norwich, r. Norwich, 20545, Private (formerly 17873, Norfolk Regiment)

JOHNSON, Edward William, b. South Pickenham, Norfolk, e. Norwich, r. Wormegay, Norfolk, 20558, Private (formerly 17986, Norfolk Regiment)

JOHNSON, Walter Goss, b. Norwich, e. York, r. Thrandeston, Suffolk, 20721, Private (formerly 18925, Norfolk Regiment)

KEMP, Tom, b. Spalding, Lincs, e. Norwich, r. Mileham, Norfolk, 20612, L/Cpl (formerly 17540, Norfolk Regiment)

KEMP, William Valentine, b. Warnham, Sussex, e. Tottenham, Middx, r. Fakenham, Norfolk, 20705, Private (formerly 3/7569, Norfolk Regiment)

KERRY, Henry, b. Scoulton, Norfolk, e. Norwich, r. Deopham, Norfolk, 20557, Private (formerly 17932, Norfolk Regiment)

KING, Thomas William, b. Bixley, Norfolk, e. Norwich, r. Norwich, 20572, Private (formerly 17828, Norfolk Regiment)

KING, William, b. Terrington Marsh, Norfolk, e. Norwich, r. Norwich, 20577, Private (formerly 17933, Norfolk Regiment)

LAKE, Horace, b. Horsford, Norwich, e. Norwich, r. Billingford, Norfolk, 20615, Private (formerly 3/10441, Norfolk Regiment)

LARKE, Charles, b. Southrepps, Norfolk, e. Norwich, r. Southrepps, 20568, Private (formerly 17934, Norfolk Regiment)

LARKE, Henry Harry, b. Norwich, e. Norwich, r. Norwich, 20671, Private (formerly 19265, Norfolk Regiment)

LEECH, James Charles, e. London, r. Bow, Middx, 20614, Private (formerly 17605, Norfolk Regiment)

LINCOLN, Charles, b. Attleborough, Norfolk, e. Norwich, r. Attleborough, 20536, Private (formerly 17937, Norfolk Regiment)

LOCKWOOD, William, b. London, e. Norwich, r. Norwich, 20613, Private (formerly 3/8155, Norfolk Regiment)

LOOME, William James, b. Pulham St Mary, Norfolk, e. Norwich, r. Pulham St Mary, 20583, Private (formerly 17939, Norfolk Regiment)

LOVATT, Arthur, b. Old Catton, Norfolk, e. Norwich, r. New Catton, Norfolk, 20670, Private (formerly 17635, Norfolk Regiment)

MAYES, Herbert George, b. Southrepps, Norfolk, e. North Walsham, Norfolk, r. North Walsham, 20709, Private (formerly 8454, Norfolk Regiment)

MEDLAR, George Stephen, b. Norwich, e. Norwich, r. Norwich, 20726, Private (formerly 18674, Norfolk Regiment)

MORTER, Arthur, b. Dilham, Norfolk, e. Norwich, r. Dilham, 20575, Private (formerly 17880, Norfolk Regiment)

MORTER, Sidney, b. Dilham, Norfolk, e. Norwich, r. Dilham, 20576, Private (formerly 17882, Norfolk Regiment)

MURIEL, Bernard John, b. Thetford, Norfolk, e. Norwich, r. North Walsham, Norfolk, 20688, L/Cpl (formerly 7273, Norfolk Regiment)

NEWSON, Basil Eric, b. Thorpe, Norfolk, e. Norwich, r. Thorpe, 20617, Private (formerly 16884, Norfolk Regiment)

NICHOLS, Herbert, b. Poringland, Norfolk, e. Norwich, r. Mundham Common, Norwich, 20730, Private (formerly 16594, Norfolk Regiment)

NICHOLS, Samuel Edward, b. Norwich, e. Norwich, r. Norwich, 20561, A/Cpl (formerly 16661, Norfolk Regiment)

NURSE, John William, b. Weybourne, Norfolk, e. Norwich, r. Weybourne, 20729, Private (formerly 16538, Norfolk Regiment)

O'CONNOR, John, b. Mansfield, Notts, e. Norwich, r. Norwich, 20594, Private (formerly 3/7709, Norfolk Regiment)

OSBORNE, Harry William, b. Wortwell, Norfolk, e. Norwich, r. Alburgh, Norfolk, 20700, Private (formerly 17134, Norfolk Regiment)

OTTY, John, b. Weybourne, Norfolk, e. Norwich, r. Weybourne, 20728, Private (formerly 15999, Norfolk Regiment)

PAGE, Harry Sydney, b. High Wych, Herts, e. London, r. Harlow, Essex, 20622, Private (formerly 12256, Norfolk Regiment)

PAGE, Jack, b. North Heigham, Norfolk, e. Norwich, r. Norwich, 20698, Private (formerly 18637, Norfolk Regiment)

PARKER, Arthur Burgess, b. Arminghall, Norfolk, e. Norwich, r. Norwich, 20560, A/Cpl (formerly 13010, Norfolk Regiment)

PARKER, Harry, b. Clippesby, Norfolk, e. Norwich, r. Great Yarmouth, Norfolk, 20621, Private (formerly 17697, Norfolk Regiment)

PARMENTER, William, b. Bethnal Green, Middx, e. Shoreditch, Middx, r. Bow, Middx, 20619, Private (formerly 18008, Norfolk Regiment)

PATTERSON, Bertie Edward, b. East Lexham, Norfolk, e. Norwich, r. Beechamwell, Norfolk, 20620, Private (formerly 17187, Norfolk Regiment)

PEACHMAN, Harry George, b. Thorpe, Norwich, e. Norwich, r. Thorpe, 20703, Private (formerly 13995, Norfolk Regiment)

PEGG, Dennis, b. Swanton Morley, Norfolk, e. Great Yarmouth, Norfolk, r. Sporle, Norfolk, 20563, L/Cpl (formerly 17811, Norfolk Regiment)

PLOWRIGHT, Sidney, b. Morley St Botolph, Norfolk, e. Norwich, r. Morley St Botolph, 20570, Private (formerly 17951, Norfolk Regiment)

PLUMBLY, Robert Samuel, b. Cromer, e. Norwich, r. Norwich, 20535, Private (formerly 17847, Norfolk Regiment)

POLLINGTON, James Henry, b. Downham Market, Norfolk, e. Kings Lynn, Norfolk, r. Mundford, Norfolk, 20707, Private (formerly 8649, Norfolk Regiment)

PRENTICE, Percy George, b. South Lopham, Norfolk, e. Norwich, r. South Lopham, 20673, Private (formerly 17571, Norfolk Regiment)

PUNT, Spencer Henry, b. Pulham St Mary, Norfolk, e. Norwich, r. Hardwick, Norfolk, 20541, Private (formerly 17799, Norfolk Regiment)

RAMM, Edward Freeman, b. Houghton, Norfolk, e. Norwich, r. Forncett St Mary, Norfolk, 20623, Private (formerly 18857, Norfolk Regiment)

READ, Samuel, b. Norwich, e. Norwich, r. Norwich, 20731, Private (formerly 3/7850, Norfolk Regiment)

READ, Sydney Alfred Frank, b. Thorpe St Andrews, Norfolk, e. Norwich, r. Panxworth, Norfolk, 20626, Private (formerly 17501, Norfolk Regiment)

REED, John William, b. Isleham, Cambs, e. Norwich, r. Southery, Norfolk, 20675, Private (formerly 17555, Norfolk Regiment)

REEVE, Albert Edward, b. Eaton, Norfolk, e. Norwich, r. Gateley, Norfolk, 20624, Private (formerly 17953, Norfolk Regiment)

REEVE, Edward Albert, b. Wymondham, Norfolk, e. Norwich, r. Wymondham, 20625, Private (formerly 17283, Norfolk Regiment)

RICHES, William John, b. Coltishall, Norfolk, e. Norwich, r. Herringfleet, Norfolk, 20556, Private (formerly 17955, Norfolk Regiment)

RICHMOND, Thomas Powyes, b. Edinburgh, e. London, r. West Smithfield, Middx, 20573, Private (formerly 18003, Norfolk Regiment)

ROBERTS, William George, b. East Harling, Norfolk, e. Norwich, r. Banham Moor, Norfolk, 20674, Private (formerly 17512, Norfolk Regiment)

ROBINSON, William Albert, b. Norwich, e. Norwich, r. Norwich, 20717, Private (formerly 3/7110, Norfolk Regiment)

ROSE, Ernest, b. Strumpshaw, Norwich, e. Norwich, r. Strumpshaw, 20722, Private (formerly 9348, Norfolk Regiment)

ROWE, George, b. Acle, Norfolk, e. Norwich, r. Acle, 20701, Private (formerly 8930, Norfolk Regiment)

RYDER, Benjamin, b. Stansted, Essex, e. Norwich, r. Cambridge, Cambs, 20540, Private (formerly 17829, Norfolk Regiment)

RYE, Ernest, b. Mileham, Norfolk, e. Norwich, r. Mileham, 20676, Private (formerly 17606, Norfolk Regiment)

SADD, William, b. Norwich, e. Norwich, r. Norwich, 20628, Private (formerly 17639, Norfolk Regiment)

SADLER, Philip, b. Norwich, e. Norwich, r. Norwich, 20680, Private (formerly 17057, Norfolk Regiment)

SECKER, Robert, b. Stradsett, Norfolk, e. Norwich, r. Fincham, Norfolk, 20555, Private (formerly 17800, Norfolk Regiment)

SKINNER, John Henry, b. Islington, Middx, e. London, r. St Pancras, Middx, 20694 (formerly 12301, Norfolk Regiment)

SKIPPER, Robert, b. Castle Acre, Norfolk, e. Felixstowe, r. Downham Market, Norfolk, 20732, Private (formerly 19194, Norfolk Regiment)

SMITH, George William, b. Lowestoft, Suffolk, e. Great Yarmouth, Norfolk, r. Great Yarmouth, 20562, L/Cpl (formerly 17839, Norfolk Regiment)

SMITH, William Arthur, b. Limehouse, Middx, e. Stratford, Essex, r. Woodford Green, Essex, 20702, Private (formerly 8315, Norfolk Regiment)

SQUIRIES, Frederick John, b. Ashwell Thorpe, Norfolk, e. Norwich, r. Wymondham, Norfolk, 20678, Private (formerly 3/10862, Norfolk Regiment)

TAYLOR, Walter, b. Norwich, e. Norwich, r. Tilney St Lawrence, Norfolk, 20629, Private (formerly 16889, Norfolk Regiment)

THIRTLE, Albert Benjamin James, b. Norwich, e. Norwich, r. Norwich, 20719, Private (formerly 3/5316, Norfolk Regiment)

THOMPSON, Dudley James, b. North Heigham, Norfolk, e. Norwich, r. Norwich, 20630, L/Cpl (formerly 17643, Norfolk Regiment)

TIPPELL, George Kent, b. Caston, Norfolk, e. Norwich, r. Bedingham, Norfolk, 20682, Private (formerly 17495, Norfolk Regiment)

TUTTLE, Edward James, b. East Tuddenham, Norfolk, e. Great Yarmouth, Norfolk, r. Great Yarmouth, 20637, L/Cpl (formerly 17596, Norfolk Regiment)

WALLIS, Reginald, b. Gaywood, Norfolk, e. Norwich, r. King's Lynn, 20683, Private (formerly 17743, Norfolk Regiment)

WARD, Fred, b. Saham Toney, Norfolk, e. Norwich, r. Saham Toney, 20550, Private (formerly 18000, Norfolk Regiment)

WATKINSON, Herbert James, b. Lambeth, Surrey, e. Marylebone, Middx, r. Paddington, Middx, 20633, Private (formerly 9413, Norfolk Regiment)

WEBB, Walter Herbert, b. Southwood, Norfolk, e. Norwich, r. Southwood, 20710, Private (formerly 17206, Norfolk Regiment)

WILLETT, Thomas William, b. Feltwell, Norfolk, e. Norwich, r. Feltwell, 20708, Private (formerly 16921, Norfolk Regiment)

WILLIAMS, Phill, b. Croxton, Norfolk, e. Norwich, r. Eccles, Norfolk, 20713, Private (formerly 16843, Norfolk Regiment)

WILLIAMSON, William, b. Gresham, Norfolk, e. Norwich, r. Gresham, 20711, Private (formerly 12066, Norfolk Regiment)

WOODS, Alfred, b. Bungay, Suffolk, e. Norwich, r. Bungay, 20684, A/Cpl (formerly 10234, Norfolk Regiment)

WOODS, David Edward Harry, b. Attleborough, Norfolk, e. Norwich, r. Attleborough, 20631, Private (formerly 17503, Norfolk Regiment)

WOODYARD, Robert, b. Weybourne, Norfolk, e. Norwich, r. Weybourne, 20727, Private (formerly 15988, Norfolk Regiment)

WORTLEY, Charles, b. Cromer, Norfolk, e. Norwich, r. Norwich, 20697, Private (formerly 16839, Norfolk Regiment)

WRIGHT, Frederick William, b. Hickling, Norfolk, e. Norwich, r. Hickling, 20543, Private (formerly 18002, Norfolk Regiment)

The King's Own Scottish Borderers – 1st Battalion

ABERCROMBIE, Henry, b. Kilsyth, Stirling, e. Kilsyth, r. Kilsyth, 14326, Private

ALLEN, Arthur, b. Leicester, e. Leicester, r. Leicester, 14553, Private

ALLEN, Michael, b. Liverpool, e. Pendleton, Lancs, r. Harpbury, Lancs, 13472, Private

ANDERSON, Robert, b. Renwick, Kirkcudbright, e. Dumfries, Dumfries, r. Durdrennan, Kirkcudbright, 14802, Private

ANDREWS, George, b. Govan, Lanark, e. Glasgow, Lanark, r. Glasgow, 7880, Private

ARMSTRONG, Archibald, b. Tundergarth, Dumfries, e. Dumfries, Dumfries, r. Tundergarth, 14828, L/Cpl

BIBLE, Frank, b. Atherton, Lancs, e. Atherton, r. Atherton, 13545, Private

BLADES, Richard, b. Stretford, Manchester, e. Manchester, Lancs, r. Stretford, 17812, Private

BROWN, David Anderson, b. Tinwald, Dumfries, e. Castle Douglas, Kirkcudbright, r. Dalbeattie, Kirkcudbright, 16338, Private

CAVERS, John, b. Hobkirk, Hawick, Roxburgh, e. Hawick, r. Hawick, 16297, Private

CHAPMAN, George Robert, b. Middlesbrough, Yorks, e. Middlesbrough, r. Middlesbrough, 7729, Private

CLARKE, Archibald, b. Leicester, e. Leicester, r. Leicester, 17817, L/Cpl

COX, Thomas Richard, b. Middlesbrough, Yorks, e. Middlesbrough, r. Middlesbrough, 7990, Private

DICKSON, James, b. Kirkbean, Dumfries, e. Dumfries, r. Dumfries, 14809, Private

DINNELL, William, b. Kirkdale, Lancs, e. Dumfries, r. Dumfries, 14805, Private

DOWDALL, John, b. Hamilton, Lanark, e. Hamilton, r. Blantyre, Lanark, 16307, Private

DOWNIE, Francis Edward, b. Gateshead, Durham, e. Glasgow, Lanark, r. Glasgow, 16227, L/Cpl

FREEMAN, Walter, b. Bolton, Lancs, e. Ashton-Under-Lyne, Lancs, r. Bolton, 11636, Private

GALLAGHER, John, b. S Leith, Midlothian, e. Leith, Midlothian, r. Leith, 16359, Private

GALLOWAY, John, b. Monkland, Lanark, e. Shotts, Lanark, r. Shotts, 13613, Private

GIBSON, Stephen, b. Blacken Point, Ches, e. Dumfries, r. Dumfries, 16210, Private

GORDON, James, b. Kirkbean, Kirkcudbright, e. Dumfries, r. Dumfries, 14795, Private

KERR, George Souter, b. Edinburgh, e. Edinburgh, r. Edinburgh, 16302, Private

KIRKPATRICK, James, b. Twynholm, Kirkcudbright, e. Dumfries, r. Twynholm, 14741, Private

LAWSON, James, b. Dysart, Fife, e. Kirkcaldy, Fife, r. Kirkcaldy, 16123, Private

LEATHER, William, b. Tyldesley, Lancs, e. Atherton, Lancs, r. Tyldesley, 13343, Private

MCCAIG, John, b. Mochrum, Wigtown, e. Port William, Wigtown, r. Port William, 16165, Private

MCGREGOR, Alexander, b. Dysart, Fife, e. Kirkcaldy, Fife, r. Kirkcaldy, 16181, Private

MCGUFFIE, Alexander, b. Mochrun, Port William, Wigtown, e. Port William r. Port William, 1667, Private

MCKAY, James, b. Aberdeen, e. Glasgow, Lanark, r. Glasgow, 16332, Private

MCMUIWIES, Joseph, b. Tynron, Dumfries, e. Dumfries, r. Dumfries, 16336, Private

MCQUEEN, Ivie, b. Dumfries, e. Dumfries, r. Dumfries, 16266, Private

MCROBERTS, Thomas, b. Bellshill, Lanark, e. Hamilton, Lanark, r. Hamilton, 16309, Private

MELVIN, Joseph, b. Whithorn, Wigtown, e. Dumfries, r. Dumfries, 16196, Private

RAMSAY, John, b. Dunfermline, Fife, e. Dunfermline, r. Dunfermline, 16315, Private

RAYNER, Henry, b. Preston, Lancs, e. Preston, r. Preston, 14563, Private

RICHARDSON, Harold, b. Crewe, Ches, e. Warrington, Lancs, r. Warrington, 17854, Drummer

RICHARDSON, Matthew, b. Lochmaben, Dumfries, e. Dumfries, r. Lochmaben, 14744, Private

SCOTT, Archibald, b. Castleton, Roxburgh, e. Hawick, Roxburgh, r. Hawick, 16126, Private

SELBY, James, b. Dundee, Forfar, e. Forres, Morayshire, r. Lochee, Forfar, 16245, L/Cpl

STEVENS, Guy, b. Broomhill, Yorks, e. Wombwell, Yorks, r. Broomhill, 13449, Private

STEWART, David John, b. Govan, Lanark, e. Govan, r. Govan, 13330, Private

TELFORD, John, b. Carlisle, Cumberland, e. Annan, Dumfries, r. Carlisle, 14742, Private

THOMSON, John, b. Kirkcaldy, Fife, e. Kirkcaldy, r. Kirkcaldy, 16268, Private

TRODDEN, Robert, b. Annan, Dumfries, e. Dumfries, r. Dumfries, 16275, Private

TURNBULL, Percy Douglas, b. Edinburgh, e. Edinburgh, r. Edinburgh, 16353, Private

WYCH, Harry Lewis, b. Stockport, Lancs, e. Stockport, r. Stockport, 16340, Private

The Border Regiment – 1st Battalion

BARNES, Thomas, b. Leyland, Lancs, e. Manchester, r. Moss Side, Manchester, 16857, Private

BARNES, William, b. Pendlebury, Manchester, e. Manchester, r. Pendlebury, 16858, Private

BARNETT, John, b. Warrington, Lancs, e. Warrington, 16923, Private

BARTON, Harry, b. Upholland, Lancs, e. Wigan, Lancs, r. Appleby Bridge, Wigan, 11747, Private

BLAKE, Arthur, b. Drewton, Yorks, e. Manchester, r. Salford, Lancs, 11937, Private

BRANNON, James, b. Dearham, Cumberland, e. Maryport, Cumberland, r. Dearham, 18000, Private

BREARLEY, James Shaw, b. Salford, Lancs, e. Manchester, r. Salford, 16579, Private

BRINDLE, James, b. Chorlton-on-Medlock, Manchester, e. Southend, Essex, r. Chorlton-on-Medlock, 19008, Private

BROUGHTON, Robert, b. Blackburn, Lancs, e. Blackburn, 16605, Private

BURNS, Thomas, b. Millom, Cumberland, e. Blackburn, Lancs, r. Millom, 14551, Private

BUTLER, Samuel, b. Farnworth, Lancs, e. Manchester, r. Farnworth, 6064, Private

CLARKE, William Henry, b. Marsh Green, Wigan, Lancs, e. Wigan, r. Marsh Green, 11808, Private

CONKEY, John Lucas, b. Clayton-le-Moors, Lancs, e. Blackburn, Lancs, r. Gt Harwood, Lancs, 26638, Private

CROMPTON, Thomas, b. Hulme, Lancs, e. Manchester, r. Hulme, 18113, Private

CROSSLEY, John, b. Manchester, e. Manchester, 16607, Private

DEANS, Edward James, b. Arthuret, Cumberland, e. Longtown, Cumberland, 19158, Private

DUTTON, Harry, b. Manchester, e. Manchester, r. Rusholme, Lancs, 16731, Private

ELLIS, Albert, b. Grasslot, Cumberland, e. Workington, Cumberland, r. Grasslot, 16732, Private

ELLIS, Thomas, b. Liverpool, e. Accrington, Lancs, r. Church, Lancs, 16714, Private

GERRARD, Frank, b. Hindsford, Lancs, e. Atherton, Lancs, r. Hindsford, 16649, Private

GIBSON, Thomas Arthur, b. Kidsgrove, Staffs, e. Wigan, Lancs, 17971, Private

GOODWIN, William, b. St Helens, Lancs, e. Manchester, r. Droylsden, Lancs, 12060, Cpl

HACKETT, Harold, b. Warrington, Lancs, e. Warrington, 16951, Private

HALL, Albert, b. Cliburn, Westmorland, e. Appleby, Westmorland, r. Cliburn, 15731, Private

HARROLD, Alfred, b. Little Hulton, Lancs, e. Farnworth, Lancs, r. Walkden, Lancs, 19215, Private

HEAD, Thomas, b. Bowsear, Penrith, Cumberland, e. Keswick, Cumberland, r. Brackenthwaite, Cumberland, 18737, Private

HENCHAN, William, b. Derby, e. Derby, 19309, Private

HICKMAN, Reginald, b. Bowden, Ches, e. Kendal, Westmorland, r. Ambleside, Westmorland, 17818, Private

HOLLAND, William, b. Bickershaw, Lancs, e. Manchester, r. West Gorton, Lancs, 16799, Private

HOWE, Albert, b. Singleton, Lancs, e. Egremont, Cumberland, r. Bowgreave, Garstang, Lancs, 19340, Private

HOWELL, John, b. Ancoats, Manchester, e. Manchester, r. Ancoats, 16870, Private

IRONS, Samuel, b. Warrington, Lancs, e. Warrington, 16954, Private

JACKSON, John, b. Cleator Moor, Cumberland, e. Cleator Moor, 19170, Private

JACKSON, Sydney, b. Rusholme, Lancs, e. Manchester, r. Rusholme, 16587, Private

JOYCE, Harry, b. Burnley, Lancs, e. Manchester, 16532, Private

KENYON, Joseph, b. Blackburn, Lancs, e. Blackburn, 16801, Private

LEE, Ernest Gill, b. Leathley, Yorks, e. Keswick, Cumberland, r. Castley, Huby, Leeds, 15848, Private

LEVIS, James, b. Salford, Manchester, e. Manchester, r. Greengate, Salford, Lancs, 6309, Private

MALONE, John, b. Wigan, Lancs, e. Wigan, 16962, Private

MATHER, Albert, b. Platt Bridge, Wigan, Lancs, e. Wigan, 17862, Private

MCBRIDE, William Hugh, b. Airdee, Lanarks, e. Whitehaven, Cumberland, r. Coatbridge, 16745, Private

MERIDITH, George, b. Swinton, Manchester, e. Manchester, r. Swinton, 16619, Private

MONKS, Edward, b. Manchester, e. Manchester, 19217, Private

MONKS, Stanley, b. Warrington, Lancs, e. Warrington, 16888, Private

MUIR, John, b. Heywood, Lancs, e. Wigan, Lancs, 17861, Private

MUTCH, Harold Thomas, b. Sault St Mary, Canada, e. Manchester, 6402, Private

NAYLOR, George Alfred, b. Bolton, Lancs, e. Bolton, 19219, Private

NICHOLSON, George Manley, b. Old Trafford, Manchester, e. Manchester, r. Prestwich, Lancs, 17743, Private

OAKDEN, Henry, b. Ardwick, Lancs, e. Manchester, 17875, Private

ORMEROD, Frank, b. Whalley, Blackburn, Lancs e. Blackpool, Lancs, r. Whalley, 12019, Private

PARKER, Joseph, b. Bolton, Lancs, e. Bolton, r. Bolton, 18318, Private

PEPPER, Joseph Edward, b. Little Langdale, Westmorland, e. Ambleside, Westmorland, r. Little Langdale, 16593, Private

PUGH, Joseph, b. Liverpool, e. Liverpool, 16966, Private

ROBEY, Richard, b. Billinge, Wigan, Lancs, e. Wigan, 11794, Private

SMITH, Sydney, b. Manchester, e. Chetham, r. Higher Broughton, Manchester, 6308, Private

THORNLEY, Albert, b. Bolton, Lancs, e. Bolton, 19188, Private

WALKERDINE, George, b. Derby, e. Barrow-in-Furness, Lancs, r. Derby, 12014, L/Cpl

WALTON, Arnold, b. Blackburn, Lancs, e. Blackburn, 16833, Private

WILLIAMS, Edward, b. Pendleton, Lancs, e. Manchester, r. Pendleton, 16698, Private

The South Wales Borderers – 2nd Battalion

ASHWORTH, Stuart, b. Bury, Lancs, e. Shaw, Lancs, 24710, Private (formerly 51309, RAMC)

ASPINALL, Robert, b. St Helens, Lancs, e. Leigh, Lancs, 24527, Private (formerly 74460, RHA & RFA)

BAILEY, John, b. Nelson, Lancs, e. Nelson, 24601, Private (formerly 57052, RHA & RFA)

BECK, Edwin James, b. Swansea, Glam, e. Brecon, Brecknock, 11657, Private

BENNETT, Stephen, b. Southwark, London, e. London, 8927, Private

BLAKEMAN, Albert, b. Fellam, Durham, e. Attercliffe, Sheffield, 35026, A/Cpl

COILS, Cornelius, b. South Hetton, Durham, e. Houghton-le-Spring, Durham, 24733, Private (formerly 45033, RAMC)

COOPER, Joseph Henry, b. Seacombe, Ches, e. Liverpool, 24571, L/Cpl (formerly 66770, RHA & RFA)

CROSSLEY, Harry, b. Birkdale, Lancs, e. Manchester, 24606, Private (formerly 67136, RHA & RFA)

CUNNINGHAM, Frank, b. Barrow-in-Furness, Lancs, e. Barrow-in-Furness, 24732, Private (formerly 46683, RAMC)

DANIELS, Henry, b. Brynmawr, Ebbw Vale, Glam, e. Merthyr, 14265, Private (formerly 7432, King's Shropshire Light Infantry)

EVANS, Philip, b. Pentyrch, Cardiff, e. Cardiff, 24938, Private

FARMER, William Thomas, b. Glyntaff, Pontypridd, Glam, e. Pontypridd, 24939, Private (formerly 62660, RFA)

GIBBS, Ernest Alfred, b. Leicester, e. Ealing, 24754, Private (formerly 51433, RAMC)

GOLDING, Frederick James, b. Bermondsey, London, e. Lambeth, London, 24570, Private (formerly 78056, RHA & RFA)

GRIFFITHS, Alfred James, b. Usk, Mon, e. Newport, Mon, 24953, Private (formerly 5202, Dragoon Guards)

HALES, Albert Edward, b. Wolverhampton, Staffs, e. Newport, Mon, 13153, Private

HARDIMAN, Walter William, b. Edgbaston, Birmingham, e. Birmingham, 24762, Private (formerly 44252, RAMC)

HARRIES, Willie, b. St Michael's, Aberystwyth, Cardigan, e. Brecon, Brecknock, 10789, Private

HART, William, b. Warrington, Lancs, e. Warrington, 19596, Private

HAYES, Harry, b. Marylebone, London, e. Cefn-Coed, Glam, 11088, Private

HICKMAN, William, b. Seacombe, Ches, e. Liverpool, 24562, Private (formerly 74538, RHA & RFA)

HOOD, Charles Henry, b. Newport, Mon, e. Newport, 19603, Private

HUGHES, John Hugh, b. Llangollen, Denbigh, e. Chester, 19797, Private (formerly 10902, Cheshire Regiment)

HUGHES, Thomas, b. Montgomery, e. Aberdare, Glam, 18748, Private

HUNTER, William, b. Leigh, Lancs, e. Leigh, 24529, Private (formerly 74561, RHA & RFA)

HURLEY, John, b. Merthyr, Glam, e. Cefn-Coed, Glam, 10967, Private

JAMES, William Robert, e. Newport, Mon, 18927, Private

KAY, Thomas, b. Warrington, Lancs, e. Warrington, 19572, Private

KNOWLES, John, b. Haydock, Lancs, e. Warrington, Lancs, 24511, Private (formerly 74931, RHA & RFA)

LEE, Wilfred, b. Nuncar Gate, Notts, e. Mansfield, Notts, 19184, Private

LEWIS, Edward, b. Abertillery, Mon, e. Brecon, Brecknock, 11802, Private

MILLS, William, b. Fenton, Staffs, e. Tunstall, Staffs, 19429, Private

MOLINEAUX, Thomas, b. Birmingham, e. Brecon, Brecknock, 15613, Private

MORGAN, Richard, b. Llanover, Blaenavon, Mon, e. Brynmawr, 10435, Private

MOSS, Edward, b. Hyde, Ches, e. Warrington, Lancs, 19630, Private

MURRAY, Samuel, b. Widnes, Lancs, c. Warrington, Lancs, 24600, Private (formerly 57191, RHA & RFA)

NIGHTINGALE, Frederick John, b. Walthamstow, Essex, e. Stratford, London, 19611, Private

NOONAN, Thomas, b. Neath, Glam, e. Neath, 24947, Private (formerly 30953, RAMC)

NUNN, Frederick Walter, b. Tottenham, London, e. Stratford, London, 10179, Sgt

PARKER, Alfred, b. St James's, Lancaster, e. Clitheroe, Lancs, 24634, Private (formerly 55956, RHA & RFA)

PEARCE, Edward, b. Risca, Mon, e. Hightown, Lancs, 25077, Private

RICHMOND, Arthur, b. Blackburn, Lancs, e. Blackburn, 24618, Private (formerly 67404, RHA & RFA)

RILEY, Patrick, b. Makerfield, Lancs, e. Wigan, Lancs, 24919, Private (formerly 43533, RAMC)

SALTER, Harry, b. Llansantffraed, Mont, e. Welshpool, Mont, 10112, Private (formerly 5438, King's Shropshire Light Infantry)

SEEL, William, b. Stockport, Ches, e. Hyde, Ches, 25506, Private

SIMPSON, George, b. Birmingham, e.
Birmingham, 19095, Private

SMITH, Albert, b. Stoke, Guildford, Surrey, e.
Hereford, 8174, Private

SMITH, Sidney William, b. Lambeth, London, e.
Canning Town, London, 24520, L/Cpl
(formerly 78434, RHA & RFA)

SPRAWSON, Albert William, b. St Martins,
Birmingham, e. Birmingham, 24809, Private
(formerly 44178, RAMC)

WARE, Sydney Stewart, b. Clifton, Bristol, e.
Bristol, 8015, Private

WEECH, Samuel, b. Bedwellty, Tredegar, Mon, e.
Newport, Mon, 14007, Private

WILLIAMS, Charles Henry, b. Salford, Lancs, e.
Salford, 19128, Private

Acknowledgements

This work has been compiled for the historic value that it may provide to my family and the small comfort it may bring to those who may still remember loved ones. During my research process many articles, features, references, quotations, postcards and photographs were discovered and used that had been published in all forms, including the world-wide web. These are many and numerous and I would like to take this opportunity to thank all of those who directly, indirectly, knowingly or unknowingly, contributed to this memorial work. Some names and acknowledgements may have been omitted simply because no trace of ownership could be found – for example, 'abandoned' websites, photographs or e-mail addresses – from text on Avonmouth and the 'Royals' to information gleaned about Coatbridge or the Fairfield yard. Therefore, to all untraced sources, please accept my gratitude: together *you* helped to make this story whole!

In particular I should like to thank the following people and organisations for their invaluable help, encouragement, permissions and input. The people of Scotland, Canada, England and Greece, Alexander and Isabella Munro, the Commonwealth War Graves Commission, Christopher J. Roberts (head of training at the Marine Society in London), Joyce Jacques, Lorna Wright, May Harvey, Trent University of Peterborough, Ontario, Canada, Martin Edwards, Terry Bracher from Northamptonshire Libraries for his list of troops, courtesy of the Navy & Military Press Ltd, Gladys Dainty of Rushton, Rear Admiral Constantine Hartofilis HCG (ret), The Nisyrian Studies Society, Paul Whitelam, www.theshipslist.com, Frank Foulds, Lester Cowling, Steve at *Sea Breezes* magazine, Thane Burnett, the *Toronto Sun*, the late Captain F. J. Thompson OBE RD RNR, Janet Peck of Burton Latimer, *Stand-To!* Journal, Letta and Ernie Lewis, Caroline and Alison Lewis, Heino J. Von Heimburg, the BBC, Martin Borley at BBCi, Zoe Kleinman from the BBC's *Ariel* magazine, the Sergeant at Arms at the Canadian Parliament in Ottawa, *Northampton Chronicle & Echo*, Ros Pates, Laura Moss, Kevin Saddington, Northants News, *Corby Evening Telegraph*, the Bristol Industrial Museum, Ian Hook from Chelmsford Borough Council, Peter Townsend and all at the Nostalgia Collection and Silver Link Publishing, David Saunders (Editor of *The Gallipolian* for the Gallipoli Association), John Harris, Don Ward, Major-General M. G. Cloutier, June Nimmo, Grainger Hill, Irene Couts, Jan Harrison, Bill Hutton, Paul Reed, Monklands Online, GWPDA, Lady Caroline Latham, Elizabeth M. Hudson, John Hayes Fisher (Producer, BBC History) Pauline Dodd (see www.geocities.com/Heartland/Acres/5564/norfolkgallipoli.html), Kate Tildesley (Curatorial

Officer at the Ministry of Defence, Naval Historical Branch), Hugh Peden, (see also http://www.pacific-pages.com/hpeden/hist002.htm), A. J. Mills (Master Masons) of Rothwell, *Crowsnest* magazine, Michelle Stavrianou, Mike Winter, Evridiki Lekati, Suzanne Fenny, Bill and Marlene McKann, the captain of the *Agious Konstantinos* (Stavrianos Nikolaos, mechanic, and George Tsoukalas, deck hand), Nikos Kalidoni, all at the Haritos Hotel in Nisyros, and all at Enetikon Travel.

And, of course, the captain, crew and all who sailed aboard the beautiful *Royal Edward*, and to Caroline Beynon for her photographic, proofreading and video skills, and for putting up with me as I tapped away on my computer.

Oh, and the cats – Archie, Rumpty, Puppin – and *all* the cats of Greece.

Index